I0504011

FAREWELL

TO NORMAL

BY

ERIC FAREWELL

FAREWELL TO NORMAL

Ordering Information: Quantity sales. Special discounts are available on quantity purchases by corporations, associations, and others. 1-800-732-9140.

www.DreamStartersPublishing.com

Table of Contents

Introduction 4

Takeoff - How to Overcome Pain and Disability 11

The Need to do More in Life 26

How to Adventure Even When You Can't Afford it 36

Reframing How to Look at the Upside 44

Truly Trust the People You Trust 53

Surround Yourself With People Who You Become Like 66

Fail Fast - Question Success 73

Leadership Within the Team 84

The Necessity of the Heart to have BIG Goals 94

The Importance of Serving Others 111

Personal Core Values 120

Doing Something Superhuman 131

Endurance; Going the Distance 139

Constant Growth 147

Pushing Past Fear and Doing What You Hate 155

Final Thoughts 164

Introduction

My name is Eric Farewell.

I am a husband, father, an adventurer, and a lover of flight. I'm a lifelong pilot, an entrepreneur, and the founder of Aviator Paramotor, a school that teaches people to overcome their fears through flight, utilizing the sport of powered paragliding, also known as paramotoring. The mission of my life and the purpose of this book is to help people realize there's life beyond fear and to realize their superhuman abilities in doing so. I believe this is something attainable for each of us, and it's a goal I was born to pursue.

I've been a pilot nearly my whole life. I was born beside a small airstrip into a close family of aviators. The passion for flight and the thirst for adventure shared by my mother, cousins, uncles, and grandparents was thusly passed to me. My first memory was at the age of three. I was in a Bellanca Super Viking, with my grandfather – a former fighter pilot and the man I most wished to emulate – at the yoke. I can still *smell* the plane and I remember every moment soaring through the sky as we barrel rolled above the orange groves below. The seed planted in my head that day continued growing throughout my adolescence and adulthood, so much so that at the age of seven I started working at my family's inn and restaurant. I bussed tables, made coffee, and helped people to their rooms for minimum wage; all of it going towards the acquisition of my first set of wings.

When I first expressed an interest in ultralights, the pilots in my family scoffed that they were dangerous, stupid, and *sure* to get me killed. But I was tenacious in my love for flying, and as a presumptuous thirteen-year-old, there was no way I could wait three more long years to "get my wings" and share in my family's adventures. Waiting until I was sixteen to solo seemed outlandish ever since the day I found out there were other options, even *with* my family discouraging them. At thirteen, my tenacity paid off. I bought my first kit ultralight. I sold it before completion, but in doing so it opened a door which led me to becoming an amateur airplane broker and flipper. I learned so much through owning and running my first business. Over the coming years I became the owner of many aircraft and the salesman of many more.

In 2012 I began another great adventure: I learned to fly paramotors. My wife had recently become pregnant with our first child. A son, August. At the time, I was flying a Cessna 140 daily to one airport restaurant or another, pulling out my laptop, to complete my day's work while watching the planes fly the traffic pattern. It was a wonderful ritual, one that kept me grounded in my passions and empowered me to challenge myself on a daily basis while meeting new, interesting people… but it was expensive, and I was perplexed, wondering how I could get my flying fix while keeping my finances in the black and of course support my growing family. Then, something revolutionized my life. At the "Sun n' Fun" fly-in that year, my attention was captivated by an amazing type of ultralight vehicle: the paramotor. The bright wings and backpack motors awed me, as did the remarkably low operating cost compared to more traditional forms of aviation. Naturally, I arranged for my lessons to begin later that very month.

Feeding the obsession that grew from my first flight under a paraglider was, thus far, the most challenging undertaking of my life, both physically and mentally. It pushed me to my limits. Never a hefty person, I still lost twenty-two pounds during my early days of training, sweat more than I knew was possible, and experienced many defeats. But I *needed* the challenge. I kept learning, kept practicing. I flew a great deal in my first year, and in short order I knew I wanted to share my love for the sport by teaching others.

I have worn many hats throughout my life. I used to make my living in marketing, business management, consulting, and strategic performance coaching, but once I discovered this new form of flight, I abandoned those ventures to pursue a new goal; sharing flight with others. I wanted the world to experience what I had – *true* flight, *true* adventure, and how to *really* feel alive. Paramotor flying filled my heart and mind in a way nothing else had. I needed to share my joy.

Thus began a huge developmental shift for me. I began to understand how I could create a more uplifting and fulfilling life by becoming more focused on serving others, impassioned with inspiring people to become the best versions of themselves they could be. I knew I could harness my growing passion for personal improvement and my love of teaching to create a school like none before it; one that not only effectively and safely taught people to fly, but one that could dramatically change our students' lives for the better.

Aviator Paramotor was born in 2012. The arduous process of building this new business nearly bankrupted our family. Twice. But I couldn't give up. Looking back now, I know if I were given the chance to go back and do it over, I wouldn't choose to walk another path in order to avoid those hardships. They helped mould me and this business into what we are today.

Today our flight school is not just about learning how to fly a paramotor, not even close. We help people look past their insecurities, overcome their pain, heal their wounds, and realize their potential for growth in all aspects of their lives. It's as much a humbling experience to better lives through this type of emotional work as it is an incredible honor.

Remarkably, our curriculum at Aviator isn't overtly structured to do this. It's a natural process born of passion, obstacles, and the presence of incredibly uplifting people. The challenges our students are presented with physically and emotionally inspire them to open up to others in the group, to share personal experiences, and to learn as a team. I have witnessed people come through our classes and workshops and completely revolutionize their very being, their sense of self, their sense of accomplishment, and their outlook on life.

This book is written in hopes you too may have a similar experience – no matter where you pursue your passions. Through these simple words, I hope you leverage your abilities to overcome your own pains, and that it helps you build greater faith in yourself. I want to share the ways I've learned to become the best version of not just myself, but also the stories of the hundreds of Aviators and adventurers who have come through my life. I'm driven to help reveal the potential in your heart, mind, and life you may not even know you have. It is my desire that through reading my experiences, you can take away something that improves your life… or at least gets you laughing at some of my adventures.

Take a leap of faith. Reach out for the unknown, live in defiance of your perceived limitations, and be prepared for your life to take flight.

"For each of them, the most important thing in living was to reach out and touch perfection in that which they most love to do, and that was to fly."

Richard Bach
Jonathan Livingston Seagull

Chapter 1

Takeoff - How to Overcome Pain and Disability

Dreams "Lost"

Two weeks before my eighteenth birthday, I hand-propped an airplane. Standing in front of the propeller, I gripped it firmly and pulled hard, physically turning the engine over by hand. Some planes don't have starter motors, so they require this. It's pretty hazardous and has been known to dismember, and even kill. But I'd been trained well and I had *plenty* of experience, at least that's what I thought. This time, however, was different. This time misfortune played her hand. The plane's engine surged to full power and took off into the side of the hangar, with an unwitting passenger clinging to the strut.

I found myself looking up at the bottom of the plane, a tire between my legs. My hands wrapped around the strut so hard I bent the metal with my fingertips. First and foremost, in my head was the knowledge that if I let go the tire was going to run me over, pushing my chest and head into the propeller, and I would die in a spectacularly unpleasant manner quite reminiscent of a *Monty Python* slasher scene.

Then, I blacked out.

Thirty odd minutes later I woke up under the plane. Blood pouring from my head, my back screaming at me in a manner of pain that was nothing short of excruciating, and I had no idea how I'd gotten there. I managed to stand up, turned the still roaring engine off, and found my way to a chair. Meanwhile, in a stroke of fortune, someone had shown up early to work at the hangar and came to investigate the noise of the plane running at full power for an overly-long time. Apparently, they ran off to call emergency services after noticing what looked like a corpse lying beneath it.

Within minutes, EMTs arrived to inform me I had a head injury. *No joke, did the blood pouring from my scalp give it away?* I thought dryly. Yet despite how much my head hurt,

I knew something else was off – in fact something else was dreadfully wrong. And I spurted out just that.

"Something's wrong with my back," I told them.

"How would you know? You have a head injury," he replied. "We need to get you to the ER to look into it."

He was far from putting my mind at ease, because there and then, I innately knew I had seriously hurt my back.

Of course, the head injury was just as real. The damage was so severe I later learned that I had lost many of my childhood memories, but that was the least of my worries. As it turned out, I had broken five vertebrae and barely skirted permanent paralysis.

When I broke my back I was left with damage that would never fully heal, including seizing back pain. My muscles would lock up, my nerves would begin firing off like an unending fireworks display, and I would be forced to the ground, frozen in pain. I remember distinctly driving through Iowa, a few months after the accident, when I began to feel the first signs of a spasm. As the fireworks began, I pulled my truck and trailer over to the side of the road, falling out and laying on the rough asphalt as my back seized, all the while tractor-trailers were unknowingly flying by my crumpled figure.

That accident shattered my life's dream and primary ambition. They precluded the possibility of me ever following in my grandfather's footsteps and becoming a fighter pilot, which had been everything I'd worked toward throughout my adolescence. As soon as the prognosis came back from the doctors I knew immediately it could never happen. The dream which had defined me for so long was lost.

My body was damaged. My identity as someone who flew disappeared like a wisp of smoke from a freshly extinguished match. Even my license plate from high school was "A8TQR" (the Q, because no one else had taken it). Flying was… me. My everything. And now it seemed I could do nothing to complete the mission I had followed for so long. Eventually though, I came to understand I had been given a choice: give up? Or move on? I was stuck with this set of circumstances, but I simply couldn't let this pain, this lost dream, destroy me or push me down. I had to let them push me *forward*.

Opportunities Found

We are all put on this earth and faced with our own special challenges almost immediately. Some of them can seem overwhelming – impossible to overcome, even. It's natural for many of us to take on the role of victim when bad news lands at our feet. But through my experiences, I learned

I had to *reframe* my hardships; to see them in a different way. Instead of reflecting on why something happened to me, I realized it could happen to someone else too, and whoever they were may be less equipped to overcome the same challenges that I was faced with.

This lesson wasn't easily learned. I once tried writing a book titled *Failing Forward* highlighting my mistakes, walking through my experiences, and how at every turn I hadn't lived up to what I had hoped. About six chapters in, I got burned out and quit.

I *failed* at writing a book about failure. The irony wasn't lost on me. But formulating the concepts in my attempt at writing a book helped me to understand that shortcomings, pain, and disappointment were not things that needed to hold me back.

As I mentioned, I worked from the ages of seven to eighteen at my grandmother's restaurant and country inn, the Chalet Suzanne. I made coffee, washed dishes, offered tours, worked as a bellhop, worked as a line cook, barkeep, and basically anywhere else help was needed. I'd always had aspirations of being an airplane owner, so I saved my minimum wage money and bought my first light aircraft kit. Inevitably it didn't take long to realize kids with ADD, ADHD, or the like (kids like myself), simply were not best suited to build (or at least finish) airplane kits. Luckily, I took a risk and attempted to sell my unfinished kit on a new thing I'd been learning about called the *internet*.

"You sold the kit thing on the interwebs?" The guy I'd bought the kit from asked me.

"Yup!" I responded proudly.

"Well, shoot, can you help me sell some of my stuff? I'll give you ten percent."

"Make it twenty," I replied with a smile.

So, at the age of thirteen, I became an amateur airplane broker. Within a couple of years, I had helped arrange the sale of more than two hundred aircraft, projects, and ultralights. I met my own goals and owned not just one plane, but had flipped over forty of my own. Lots of airplanes came into my life, including the one I had the fateful accident with.

Moving On

A few years after the accident, still trying to find myself after losing my fighter pilot dreams and freshly heartbroken from a relationship that ended poorly, I decided I *needed* an adventure, so I started planning a grand one. I had a friend who would eventually become the best man in my wedding, Ethan Demme, who wanted to ride his motorcycle to Alaska – of *course* I had to join him – but Alaska wasn't enough. We needed to do something bigger. So, we rode our motorcycles across the country, from Florida to Pennsylvania, back to Tennessee, through the great plains, to Canada and Alaska, down to San Diego, then back home again. We called it "The Bow Tie Tour" (bowtietour.com), as we crisscrossed the nation.

As if our road trip wasn't exciting enough, in the process of trekking North America I had two more serious accidents that totaled my bikes and resulted in even more broken bones. Through intense pain, I kept going. I knew I needed to experience life in a fulfilling, adventurous way once again. I needed to push myself forward, past what I saw as *my failure*, to become victor rather than victim.

We ended up riding through Alaska in the middle of what they called their "forty-year storm," a terrible weather pattern which occurs every half century or so. It rained so heavily bridges began washing out, and we forded those flooded bridges, water rushed past our feet as we crept across. One full day of riding led us only eight miles down the road – exhausted and soaked to the bone – we found shelter at a lodge that proudly proclaimed, "No Vacancy." At that point, "no" wasn't an answer we could possibly take, so I asked other guests if we could crash on their floor… and somehow it worked! In fact, it ended up working out a lot better than we expected – or rather, I should say it worked out quite unexpectedly. Not only did we secure a place to sleep in the lodge (on kind strangers' floors), but we found ourselves with the cast and crew of the movie *Into the Wild*, sharing fishbowl-shaped (and -sized) beverages and laughing as Sean Penn bantered on about his political beliefs, hotly debating anyone who dared disagree with him.

It was then I realized I was once again, *truly* alive. Our ridiculous situation really helped me understand how I had overcome adversity, shifted gears, found new goals, a new mission, a new calling, and *forced* my way forward.

How we approach our own pain or perceived disabilities is either a way to make excuses, or a way to redirect our lives. I was fortunate enough to have the support around me to help me take my pain and disability into a redirect. It allowed me to live in twenty-seven different places in a five-year timespan. It allowed me the freedom to live a really unique lifestyle; doing things like surfing in the Pacific's cold waters so long it took an hour for the feeling to return to my hands before I could unzip my wetsuit or flying halfway across the country in an ultralight at the age of sixteen.

Sometimes we have to choose to accept, even *seek* discomfort, instead of believing it is a disability. Choosing to look at pain or a physical/mental challenge as nothing more than a simple discomfort and then *choosing* to live in spite of it is crucial to overcoming yourself – along with the obstacles set in your path.

For fifteen years I'd lived in constant pain from my first accident, and the ones that followed it. In 2019 I finally decided I'd had enough. It was time for surgery.

In my first consultation, they asked the standard questions, beginning with: "What is your pain scale from one to ten, one being little to no pain, and ten being severe?"

I sat back and thought about it a bit, then replied honestly, "I think between six and seven."

I underwent a myriad of tests, including a particularly tortuous series of MRIs of my back. Soon after, I was notified I had broken five vertebrae (not the four I was originally told when the accident occurred) and two more in another incident. To top it off, I had five badly herniated discs, and scoliosis. But then, they told me something that shifted my understanding of pain:

"You say you're living with a pain level of six or seven, but based on the damage done to your back, and the resulting permanent nerve damage, you're really more likely living with a pain scale of nine out of ten," the doctor explained. "When you're in so much pain you can't pick up your kids, can't breathe, can't function normally, *that's a problem*."

Shedding "Disabilities"

Too often we choose to frame things as a problem instead of saying, "It's just what I have to deal with – what else am I going to do with my life?" I choose what I need to do to go further, to make myself a better person, to move forward in a way that helps me help others.

The cards we are dealt are just our starting point. We never *have* to choose to accept that those cards define us. Instead, we can choose to believe they help us define our own success and our own abilities. At the end of the day, if you let yourself, or someone else, limit your potential, you are shortening your own life – maybe not in literal terms as far as how long you physically live, but certainly in a way that diminishes your potential to live fully and enjoy your life.

I was a nerdy, sickly-looking child. I've always been thin, and when I was young, I was diagnosed with bronchial spasms. Not to be taken lightly, my attacks were extremely dangerous (like, rush to the hospital if you lost your inhaler, dangerous). But, aside from the attacks, it never felt like it limited me until I was thirteen. I was on Catalina Island (off the southern California shore, in the Pacific Ocean). A magnificent place for all water sports, it was especially grand for scuba diving among the wonderful kelp forests of the nature preserves around the island.

When the diving crew discovered I had asthmatic symptoms, I was told, "No way! You can't scuba dive!" I wasn't even given a chance. Instead of helping me work through the physical reality of having issues with my lungs, helping me control my breathing so I didn't hyperventilate, they simply put a stop to me sharing the dream I had of breathing underwater with the rest of my family. Too often society is like this – we are told by others (who usually mean well), what we *can't* do. It's up to us to find a way to push those hesitations to the side and figure out for ourselves what we *can* do and what we *want* to do in order to find a safe solution to society's normalcy. Today, I *love* scuba diving thanks to a friend who took the time to help me reframe my struggles and showed me that even despite my challenges, I could learn to come alive underwater.

After breaking my back, and losing my memory, I found new ways to feel like I was living: surfing, video games, racing motorcycles, taking myself on adventures around the world. It wasn't that I wanted to do things only for myself; it all parlayed into wanting to help others. For example, I enjoyed the video game *Call to Duty,* and played a lot right as it became in vogue as a spectator sport. I loved watching people play online, however I also believed my message of "truly living," of really feeling alive, could help kids see there was more to life than just gaming alone. Through my desire to reach people I decided to start making video. The very first video I made was a mix of me playing *Call of Duty* and another one of my airborne-based activities – skydiving. I wanted to show how being fully engaged as a human was empowering. Whether flying, falling, or enjoying an online game, this engagement was imperative to me, especially after observing that there was a massive community of young people following "video game personalities," people who recorded themselves playing and then put their videos on YouTube. I thought it crucially important to inspire them to grow from within, to meet them at their interests, but to show them there really is more life to be lived. That remaining stagnant playing games and watching YouTubers without any deeper engagement limited their potential… they were meant for *more.*

Flying

People come to our flight school because they have a dream. Maybe they watched "some kid," like my prior student, dear friend, and member of our Paradigm Aerobatic team, Tucker Gott, fly to McDonald's on YouTube, or perhaps they've given up a lifelong love of airplanes after starting their families. They see flying as the ultimate source of freedom, and they see taking flying lessons as a way to achieve a moment of being whole. When they walk in the door they know they're in for a change, but in truth, they have no idea how great a change it might be.

Our first two-hour session sets the foundation for everything we do at Aviator. We spend time getting to know each other's stories, along with our motivations for being there. Each student's story is important to us, as is sharing the histories of our instructors and staff – showcasing their humanity beyond just their passion for flight. We explain at the end, however, that people come to this class because flying is our "hook," but *there's so much more* that can come out of the experience.

Life is like that. Lived fully it's not just a series of days you trudge through. There's so much more available to you than checking things off of a bucket list or taking your annual vacation. After only a short time of being a part of our class, each band of new Aviators becomes a real family. They triumph together, struggle together, and relentlessly work towards perfecting their skills as a whole. Things are often shared, which haven't been shared with many others – struggles. They've either already overcome their struggles or are actively growing through them. Old pains are shared as easily as the laughter that comes from new strains and bruises. It's something each student experiences when they get their start.

There are times in our lives when we need people around us to remind us of who we are meant to be – for me that was my wife. Nelle, has been there for me through my biggest moments of doubt (even the many moments that surrounded writing this book; Was I willing to bare my soul? Was my message worthy of reading?). Classmates, or wingmen as we call them in our flying school, become those people to their fellow students. Sometimes it takes adversity, and a reminder from others that ***being afraid of hurting yourself is sometimes more crippling than actually hurting. Being afraid of living is more crippling than death.***

"Once you have tasted flight, you will forever walk the earth with your eyes turned skyward, for there you have been, and there you will always long to return."

Leonardo da Vinci

Chapter 2

The Need to do More in Life

I was blessed to have entrepreneurial parents. When I was three years old, they started a business that sold books to homeschoolers. This was long before Amazon and the advent of massive internet sale sites, so we traveled half the year from the time I was three to eighteen, first in a small TransVan, and eventually in a bus originally owned by the Charlie Daniels Band. We crammed five children and two adults in that coach and explored all America had to offer. Behind us we towed 22,000 pounds of books to homeschool conferences across the United States, nearly every weekend, six months each year.

We would all unload and reload those books and travel as a family in-between. On the weekends we had free, my father would find an adventure for us. Whether it was trout fishing in the mountains of New Mexico, or working at a dairy farm in Wisconsin, he would find some way for us to experience something more in life.

When I was fifteen, we read a book called *Wild at Heart* by John Eldredge. We all read a lot – and I've always been an obsessive reader – in fact, we didn't even have television growing up. Reading was our escape. But this book was particularly influential on my dad, and ultimately on me. Eldredge talks about man's desperate need to do something adventurous, to do something that pushes their boundaries and encourages them to live beyond their normal, comfortable state.

Life is not meant to be lived in comfort. We are meant to enjoy our comforts, certainly, but *real life* is not lived in those comfortable places. Being able to push yourself beyond comforts and into adventure is everything, according to Eldredge.

From the day we read that book, I chose to live my life by making sure every decision involved the question:

How can I make myself uncomfortable?

The history of my business reflects this; I went from being a sole proprietorship, to being in a partnership, to buying out my partner and stepping away from most of my everyday duties managing the company. I moved into a place where I could focus on keeping the culture we'd developed thriving and worked harder to inspire more people to follow their heart into flight. I've maintained my role of founder and president of Aviator, but I had my team take over much of the job that had kept me away from my family for more hours each week than I care to admit. It was a super uncomfortable shift for me initially. It changed everything about my life. I liken the situation to a homeowner moving from the position of working *on* the property like a groundskeeper to slowly realizing that, as he hires more and more of the right people, his role transitions to that of the "owner of the manor;" he's there to inspire and to show the value of the work, but is in a position which now focuses on other things as the new groundskeepers do what they were hired to do.

So, in the wake of this change, the question was "What am I going to do with my time at this point in my life?" It started with writing this book, sharing my experiences, because I'd seen what a difference my choices made in helping others follow a similar path. But after that? I was going to make myself uncomfortable again and let other people, who were better at my old job's roles, take them over. I'd step back and plan another adventure to grow myself further.

Making Mistakes – Learning from Adventure

I'm far from unique in my family – the whole foundational element of my family's beliefs is that it's okay to fail. It's okay to make mistakes (as long as we learn from them). The easiest way to make smart mistakes, and learn from them, is by putting ourselves into difficult or challenging situations, so we can grow and become better people.

When my father read *Wild at Heart*, and subsequently shared it with our family, we were in Colorado Springs. We stayed with our "cousins," the Irwin-Ewing family...we'd been intertwined with the Irwin's for longer than I've been alive.

Just days after finishing the book, my father, my brother, Joseph, a few of the Irwins, and I went hiking up a mountainous valley near where we were staying. The hike was alongside a wonderful creek, we could hear the bubbling water, the wind in the tall aspen trees, and the melody of the birds flying above. We hiked and fished, casting our Mepps double ought lures into the water in hopes of a bite from a rainbow trout. Steadily we made our way down the trail, until we finally reached a small ghost town on the shores of a small lake. We took our packs off and camped there for the night.

Having successfully caught several fish throughout the day's stream-led hike, we had just enough for dinner after settling into our campsite. All we had were those fish, and the jerky and granola bars we brought with us. We were living from the land. It was an incredible moment in time for fathers and sons, spending idyllic time together on our own private adventure.

Truth be told, though, I started out terrified. *We're going to hike miles up, hopefully catch some fish, and that's all we'll have to eat – we'll camp there overnight, and then hike how many miles back!?* I recall thinking, incredulously. But that adventure, along with the lessons I learned from Eldredge's book and my dad, have stayed with me throughout my life.

It's not enough to live, going through the motions, and following the "rules" society puts on us. To truly live, we have to overcome adversity, sometimes creating our own sort of adversity via adventure. Have you ever noticed how similar those words are? Adversity and adventure? The definition of adversity, though different than adventure, *leads* into it. Overcoming a difficulty, an adverse situation, leads to an adventure. The root word of adventure is the Latin, *adventus*, meaning *"to arrive."*

To adventure is to arrive; at your true potential, to your meaning in life. To me, adventure is taking on something bigger than yourself. It's doing something you're not sure you can accomplish and choosing to believe you will. You make the choice to have the faith and confidence in yourself – that it's something you can not only manage, but something you will *overcome.*

Flying Through Storms

A few years ago, a very dear friend came to me. Her husband had unexpectedly filed for divorce and she needed to pick up her airplane from their home in California. The next day, we airlined to San Francisco and then hopped in a small plane, a Cessna 150 Aerobat, and spent the next three days (29.6 hours of flight time) flying across the United States, from Central California, back home to Florida.

She's an incredible pilot. At the time she was a member of the US Unlimited Aerobatic team, an airshow pilot, and a true legend in the world of inspiring women aviators. She worked hard to help me learn as much as possible, to challenge me, and to help me better define good decision making. We persevered through long hours, late nights, crazy weather and at one point in our trip, while trying to transition through Dallas, we tried to outrun a thunderstorm. The intensity was so great it was like the storm was attempting to pull us into its raging air. Engine at idle, flaps down, diving away, we barely made it out. Finally landing just west of the city where we spent the night, we watched an incredible lightning display generated from the storm that earlier tried to suck us into oblivion.

Those moments of trepidation in the air with my friend and the desire to learn from our experience have never left me, just like the fishing trip with my dad will never leave me either. I've experienced these types of adventures countless times throughout my life. And I will continue to, as long as I still choose the hard things. The things that challenge me as a person.

To me adventure ultimately manifests itself as something that pushes us, maybe even makes us feel afraid, but is something we *believe* we can overcome.

I believe adventure makes you mentally stronger and wiser. I believe we are largely defined by the experiences and adventures we've had. Adventures also allow us the opportunity to seek out mentors who have succeeded through their own adventures as well. We find things that bring us joy and fulfillment, so we can fill our own cups of need in life. Only then can we help fill the cups of others.

Overcoming something – whether it's adversity or a disability – helps us build confidence, so we can continue on our adventures, so we can continue to arrive in this life of ours. These adventures can and do change lives, we see it every day at our flight school. Witnessing people change through these experiences is beyond addicting, so much so, that everyone who works at our schools has made significant lifestyle sacrifices in order to work with us. Almost every one of our instructors has worked at the top of their fields, but they've taken pay cuts, oftentimes foregoing much more within this lifestyle shift, all so they can experience what it feels like to help someone else achieve their goals. But, when you see the face of a student who has just landed a paramotor for the first time – oftentimes their eyes leaking, sometimes weeping – you'll never get a deeper sense of joy, of pride, in knowing you helped them defy what seemed to be an impossibility in taking on the skies by themselves. Simultaneously, and most importantly, the students are *always* changed for the better.

"I just stole moments in Heaven."

One of our students could not have exemplified this better, even if he tried. Being a big, burly guy from Montana with a bushy beard to go along with his image, he'd spent many a day adventuring in the rugged backcountry. Yet when he landed from his first flight, his face streaked in tears, he breathlessly declared, "I just stole moments in Heaven."

Likewise, another paramotoring friend, who had lost his daughter a few years before, landed, wide-eyed, exclaiming, "I just got to fly with my daughter."

Fondly, my dad – who I was blessed to share the joy of teaching only two years after I learned to fly myself – likes to say, "I don't just get to see the sunset, I get to be *in* the sunset. *I get to be a part of it!*"

All of these are expressions of people feeling and living their own personal nirvana; a peaceful place of satisfaction and accomplishment. All of these "stolen moments from Heaven" seem literal when you're experiencing flight, but I believe they can be accomplished no matter what your adventures are, no matter where you come from, or how you arrive.

"Life is either a daring adventure or nothing."

Helen Keller

Chapter 3

How to Adventure Even When You Can't Afford it

Adventures come from the heart, not the pocketbook. The concept of what you can afford is not just monetary. You have to look at what you can afford as both the concept of time, as well as emotionally and socially. Most people stop themselves from taking adventures, from doing things that build them up, because they're either afraid of the monetary risk, or they're afraid of what the impact will be on those they love.

What Is Your Adventure?

My wife once had an experience with a therapist, where she was told to write down anything she would do if she wasn't afraid of hurting someone else or compromising any of her relationships. What would she do if she didn't have to worry about how her actions impacted her loved ones? No matter the activity. No matter what the item was. If she knew it wouldn't impact anyone except herself, what would she do? My wife found this to be a profoundly challenging, yet thought-provoking activity so she asked me to make a similar list.

I spent weeks agonizing, trying to figure out what I would write, because at first I honestly couldn't think of anything I would do. However, when I finally put pen to paper, I wrote, and wrote, and wrote. In minutes, I had over thirty items on my list, and these weren't just things I wanted to do; these were things I would definitely do if I didn't have to worry about how it would impact everyone else in my life.

Some of the things I listed were concrete and easy to "check-off," like wanting to travel more, or wanting to spend more time in the woods, to be surrounded by mountains. Other things were more "abstract," like leaving a legacy of love and service, or being a good leader, or to build something that brought honor to my family's name. I also wrote down that I wanted to do "guy things" with my boys – to teach them to fish and hunt – like my father did for me; and I wanted to show my daughter how much I loved her and how valuable she was in ways she would remember for the rest of her life. I wanted to help my wife grow through her traumas. I wanted to grow my business so I could bless more people (without hurting my work/life balance).

Some of these activities might require me to be away from my family – like spending more time in the mountains. I feared I might let someone down. But, the reality I know now is that if I create time in my life to achieve those goals and activities, I can come back so much more fulfilled, and so much more able to serve them.

Epic Travels

On the monetary side, I commonly hear people claim there's no way they can adventure since they simply do not have the funds. When I hear this, I think back to my "Bow Tie" motorcycle trip to Alaska. At the time, I had barely enough money for the motorcycle, let alone take the trip. Two weeks before we were set to leave, a friend and I crashed into each other on our motorcycles. It totaled my Yamaha FZ-1, breaking my tibia and fibula, while also tearing my PCL. All the money I had saved up for the trip, instead, had to go toward hospital bills and getting my own motorcycle replaced. But, I also knew I had to do this trip – *I had to make it happen.* So, I asked my friend Ethan (and future best man) to help me out. We put the damages on his credit card, and I promised to pay him back.

We both took a financial risk to go on this adventure – and, it was worth it! – a trip of a lifetime. The price I paid monetarily was a temporary situation. The price I paid physically, by going on a motorcycle trip with a busted-up knee, is that I now have a weathervane for a joint. When it rains, I often have a bit of a limp. But, far more importantly, I have hundreds of amazing memories with unforgettable stories to go along with each one. In short, I was in pain, out of money, but knowing I had set aside the time to do something that was going to be truly life changing.

I knew it was all worth it when we were coming out of the town Whitehorse, in the Yukon Territory, of Canada. I remember cresting a ridge, the sunset seeming to race toward us, with evergreen trees as far as the eye could see as they began rising into a rose-colored sky. In what felt like a never-ending sunset, it was like riding straight into Heaven. Every single ounce of pain, frustration (and eventually carpal tunnel in both wrists), was worth it.

I rode tens of thousands of miles on my motorcycles that year, but if I was able, could I do it again physically, financially, or otherwise? I was nineteen then, before marriage, children, and growing a larger business. I'm not sure if I could or would do such a trip again. The more important thing is that I *experienced* it; scraping by financially, sure, camping by the road, enjoying the kindness of strangers, and adventuring. We hiked to scenic vistas, befriended fellow riders, overcame major obstacles, and skipped stones off mountain ponds few have ever seen...

Arriving – to the people we were designed to become.

Fulfillment as Adventure

For me, it comes down to what brings you fulfillment. If you don't do those things you love, are you ever really going to be happy? Things that make you feel like there's more to life, feed your soul and spirit, and that allow you to be more available to those you love. If you don't take the effort and time – whether it's picking up a side hustle so you can finally take to the skies, the roads, or the water, or if it's planning a personal get away to get back in touch with what truly brings you joy – you cripple yourself. It stands for all of us, we cripple who we were meant to be.

There's a cost for doing nothing, which is bigger than the cost of doing something that brings you fulfillment, satisfaction, and feeling like you're truly alive. You will pay the price with your most precious commodity... your life.

Adventure can be found anywhere and anytime. You don't have to take a ridiculous motorcycle trip around the continent. It can be in everyday activities, as long as it's pushing you out of your comfort zone. If you're learning a new language, it means trying it out by asking directions or getting into conversation with someone who speaks this new language better than you do. If the activity makes you feel like you're pushing yourself to be a better person; a smarter person, a more well-rounded person, a person who is taking a risk, you are doing life *right*.

When you choose discomfort over normalcy and you are willing to push yourself in body, mind, and spirit to develop who you are, you can finally develop into your full potential. So many people live life in fear, they don't ever *really* live.

With all that being said, think about what you would do if it wouldn't hurt anyone else around you – even if you think it might – just once explore the possibility of "what if?" The sky's not even the limit, what adventure would you pursue? What new thing would you try? What old hobby would you return to? What overall lifelong legacies could you possibly achieve? Focusing on your growth and happiness. Taking time away from your family, time away from your work, and *really considering how you can serve them better* by fulfilling a life purpose of your own. Breathe. And write your thoughts below.

Make your own list here:

_____

_____

_____

"Once you replace negative thoughts with positive ones, you'll start having positive results."

Willie Nelson

Chapter 4

Reframing. How to Look at the Upside

One of the constructs of who I am, which has allowed me to have the success I've had, is the fact that I never hold onto the feeling of failure. I never allow myself to focus on the bitterness. I never allow myself to hold on to the experience of something negative – instead, I want to learn from it quickly, catalog the knowledge, and then *press on*.

Fail fast. Move on. And learn from the next thing.

Understand what happens when you fail; but don't focus on it. Don't emphasize it. Learn and move on. Learn and grow through it.

Like anyone, I've had relationships fail, business ventures bomb, and accidents and mishaps within my life and career. I have had many losses, but the one that most stands out is losing my baby brother, James, in a car accident in 2018. It is one of the greatest tragedies of my life. He was just twenty-two with a son, only a few months old.

We all have loss, we all experience terrible grief. It's that grief, that loss, which helps us understand who we are and who we can be. These tastes of tragedy should influence us to truly savor the *good* in life.

Sometimes the difficulties are tragic as much as they are terribly inconvenient. It was three years after starting Aviator and I was doing all I could to keep the business from falling apart. I was working with James, putting in ninety plus hours a week. Our entire lives revolved around the business; we even had students staying in my family's home. My wife and I were expecting our third child, Eloise. We didn't have health insurance, so we were placed in a Medicaid program and though we never knew they were included, were given food stamps for a three-month period.

I'll never forget the feeling of getting that first food stamp card in the mail, where we were told we had $450 a month for food. At the time, Nelle was feeding our family of four on just under $30 a week – we were living on beans, ramen, and rice. Though we stayed positive and tried to set an example for our two boys, we named one of our favorite recipes "fancy ramen," which was a plain ramen noodle pack topped with cilantro, carrots, and spices.

Despite the struggle, it was with the help of those food stamps that I finally built up the confidence to invest *everything* we had left into the business. We took bigger risks than we ever would have otherwise.

It was during this time another friend of mine , Travis Burns, stopped by to see what Aviator was all about. He was mostly curious about our curriculum and methods of teaching. After a week of him visiting, helping out, and encouraging our methods, I told him, "You can't leave – you have to be here, working with me." But he had just retired from the Coast Guard, and was currently on a long-awaited RV vacation with his family. They were only supposed to be making a short detour at Aviator before heading out to see the Redwoods, which they'd planned on for years.

His visit ended and they departed as intended. Five hours into their trip west, Travis turned his life around after speaking with his wife. He knocked on my office door, surprising the heck out of me with his presence. They wanted to go for it – to take a chance on Aviator, on us – and ended up purchasing a house nearby. A year later, Travis became my business partner and with his help we began doing all we could to build our business.

We worked hard for four years together to build the sport of paramotoring, to promote it to the masses, and to make our training safer and more professional than ever. But the added growth had a negative side effect – many other schools started popping up, run by part-time, new instructors who didn't have their hearts as focused on service. Their clients frequently complained to us about how they had expected "Aviator-level service" from the other flight schools they attended, but never received it.

Hearing their pleas, even after our years of non-stop effort, we finally came to a resolution at the end of 2018. Everyone involved with Aviator agreed we had to scale and grow so we could provide our unique services to more people.

A few months later however, Travis realized he didn't really want to work in a company scaling at our level. His desire was to *finally* enjoy retirement with his family. Growing in order to serve those who were hurt by going elsewhere showed us that there was an incredible amount of work to be done. It also highlighted that this endeavor would involve a lot more pressure than before. By comparison, we'd been running a relatively hobby-esque business up until that point. So, rightfully, he decided to leave and *finally* retire.

At first, there was a massive feeling of abandonment, of rejection. But soon after, with just a bit of time, I realized the real power of what Travis did. He helped me get our business to the place where we could even consider scaling upward – as we have since that turning point. He worked to put systems in place and refined details we hadn't considering previously. With those systems, we could actually "plug-and-play" our operations in order to scale upwards. With those systems, I could make decisions quickly and follow the advice of my mentors; I could do so much more in, on, and for the business.

My family, along with Aviator, went through a lot to say the least. From being put on food stamps, to having a partner who helped build business every year, to losing that partner yet still moving the business forward , we ended up going from four to over twenty employees within the year following our decision to scale. The pressures of being broke helped me see where I needed help. From there, Travis aided us in getting to a place where we could be financially and emotionally successful in a scalable way.

There truly was a silver lining to the dark cloud, even if I didn't see it at first. But in life – as with flight – everything is possible when you choose to see above the clouds.

Moving Beyond Bitterness

As we go through life, we experience mishaps, loss, and grief. Indeed, it's a part of life. We lose someone we adored. We get fired from a job we loved. People we care about move away. Our favorite pets die. There are so many reasons to be overwhelmed by the atrocities our lives bring us. But, if we can move beyond the bitterness of the pain of those types of experiences, we can see how sweet life really is.

My wife and I have spent a fair share of our energy on major health kicks throughout the years. Doing all we can to better our bodies, minds, and spirits. Encouraged by mentors, we went through an unusual cleanse, Nelle being the first to dive in.

"UGH, you'll hate it – it's *terrible!*" she warned me, pointing to the empty glass of Epsom salt solution she'd just downed.

Oh well, I thought to myself. *I have to get through it.* So, I quickly chugged my own glassful, thinking even more quickly, *okay, that is bitter*.

To cleanse my palate, I followed it up with a glass of fresh tap water. Immediately shocked, I couldn't believe how delightful this plain old glass of water tasted. It was like sweet ice melt from a glacial lake mixed with honeysuckle and happiness. Far outweighing the bitterness of Epsom salts, this water tasted sweeter than I ever imagined water could taste.

Only after the pain of tasting bitterness in our lives, can we truly feel and taste the sweetness of life. When we are coasting along, not reflecting on our pain and hurt – only collecting it – we lack the ability to taste the fresh sweetness that is *real* living. Normal, everyday little things, like a fresh glass of water after ingesting something so deeply bitter, can reframe our expectations. In reframing those expectations, we can actually become empowered to see the beauty of the mundane.

Reframe to Positive

Reframing is best described as looking at all of the negatives that happen to you and finding ways for them to become positive experiences. When my brother, James, passed away, I was the one who had to call my parents and siblings and break the terrible news to them. To share his loss with his mother, father, siblings, and his girlfriend, the mother of their child, was without a doubt, the hardest thing I have ever had to do. Parents don't ever expect to outlive their children. Older siblings never expect to outlive their younger sibling. Slunk down on the steps of an emergency stairwell, I made my late-night calls. Weeping with each of those who loved James, I remember each word, each sound, from every person I spoke to. I feel the bitterness of those hours in all that I am.

Over the next few days, I saw how people hurt – people all around us, people who barely knew my brother, because they saw our pain. There's no way to instantly accept such a loss and immediately find any joy in it. However, I will say it brought our family together, and *that* was a beautiful thing. We have a renewed joy in how we see each other, and how we value not just each other, but all of those we love.

Being willing to take the time in your life to focus on the positive – not to ignore the negative – but, to find a way you can inspire others through it, is everything. There are really only two roads to go down when tragedy strikes, or when your life is interrupted by something genuinely hurtful. You can go down the road where everything, from that point on, tastes bitter; or you can take the road where you see the sweetness in what remains, and from there build a new life, a new perspective, a new pathway that streams out in all directions – directions you could never see from the dark path of bitterness and anger.

It might feel trite, especially after tragedy hits, but choosing joy, and not to live in the natural mire of sadness that comes after heartache, allows you to feel the joy you would otherwise miss. There have been times my personal pain has come from holding onto emotions, instead of letting myself feel them fully. It's important to know your true self, and to find ways to better that self in the face of difficult times.

"Trust is the glue of life. It's the most essential ingredient in effective communication. It's the foundational principle that holds all relationships."

Stephen R. Covey

Chapter 5

Truly Trusting the People You Trust

When I was sixteen, I went to my first real marketing conference. It was put on by Armand Morin, in San Francisco. My father took me to this conference specifically designed for people who wanted to sell information products on the internet. It was a whole new world at the time; how to market yourself and your services using long tale-sales copy.

At the event, I heard a man speak named Alex Mandossian – he had developed a Socratic marketing style he called, "The Ask System." The name may sound overly simple, but it was a brilliant presentation, if not the best of the entire conference.

Since I was still a kid, Alex didn't mind that I was following him around like a puppy dog. I carried his books, his bag, got him coffee, and practically begged him to mentor me.

He might have felt sorry for me, but he looked at me and said, "Ok, Eric. Let's do this." And, he didn't let me down.

For the next several years, he showed me the ropes and how I could succeed in whatever I wanted to do when it came to pretty much any entrepreneurial exercise. In fact, when I was still a teenager, I stayed with him and his family (in their garage, turned guest room) for a whole month, and received a truly "intensive" time of training fine-tuning my natural sales and business skills.

Beyond the marketing expertise Alex showed me, what I learned, which is even more important I think, is that there are certain people who come into your life who are smarter than you. Alex was (and is) so much more brilliant than I am on so many subjects and on so many levels. While he was unforgettably one of my first, since shadowing Alex I've spent my entire adolescent and adult life surrounded by incredible mentors.

Learning From and Trusting Mentors

I'm almost always working with several mentors who have much more wisdom, experience, and perspective than I could ever construct alone. When I connect with a mentor who is very successful, I don't have to understand "why" they are successful, or "why" what they say to do works – my pattern has just been to follow their experience and do what they say to do. Whenever I've trusted this, it has almost always worked well for me. If I spent all my time and effort attempting to understand the minutiae of the "why," I'd never have the energy required to actually *implement*.

Instead of using my time and energy attempting to fully understand, I choose to take that time and focus on bettering who I need to be, while following the wisdom of those who have gone before me.

This is not to say the minutiae isn't valuable. When you're learning to fly a plane, or sail a boat, knowing the physics behind how the air passes over and under the wing or past the sail helps you understand how you can control speed, direction, ascent/descent, etc. But, only to a point. If you get hung up on the "trivial" details, you might miss the bigger picture. Worse yet, you may spend so much time and energy chasing down understanding, you'll never actually experience the joys of completing the tasks at hand. Life – like flying – is often about more art, than science. When you spend your life focused on understanding every moment logically, you often lose the beauty of the art that surrounds you.

Flying With an Expert

When you learn to fly with a mentor at your side – whether the flying is literal, or symbolic of your entrepreneurial or life adventures – you can feel comfortable in your experience. There's someone at your side who will help you when needed, and while a great mentor lets you make mistakes so you can learn from them, they also keep your safety as a paramount concern.

In addition to trusting others, learning to trust that you don't have to be the one who's the expert in everything you do is also crucial. Instead, focus on what you love. If you spend your life trying to become the best accountant you can be for your company when you hate bookkeeping and numbers, you're never going to feel like you have an empowered life.

For me, it meant giving up my role as the operations manager of Aviator, so I could focus on what I love and what makes me feel truly alive: traveling, and showing people what an adventurous life can look like. Instead of sitting at my desk, looking at spreadsheets and reports, I'll spend my Mondays jumping off cliffs, riding motorcycles, or flying paramotors and bush planes to places few have been. I'll take the time to go exploring with my sons, venturing into places where I can teach them to fish for their own rainbow trout. I will take my daughter on dates or take extra time each morning to dance with her, smiling big because her laughter at my antics fills my ears.

Giving something up that didn't bring me life was my next step. What's yours?

How do You Find People to Trust?

A lot of elements go into finding people you can trust. How do you find the right mentors? And, how do you establish meaningful relationships with the people who can guide you? Unless you're a teenager with a large amount of ADD and a laughable lack of normal social skills, you probably aren't going to simply attend a conference and land your dream mentor right out of the gate.

Malcolm Gladwell wrote a book I read when I was about nineteen called *Blink: The Power of Thinking Without Thinking*. When I say this book transformed me, it's a bit of an understatement. Becoming aware that our subconscious mind knows more than we give it credit for, as outlined by Gladwell, was a huge game changer for me.

By following your subconscious first, and trusting your gut, you will almost always go in the right direction. Of course, sometimes you'll be wrong. However, Gladwell illustrates when you're looking for a mentor who shares your values and vision for what you want the world to look like, you'll often be steered in the right direction by listening to what your subconscious mind is trying to tell you.

Choose mentors who are *already* successful in what you want to do. If they aren't successful, they have no business telling you what to do when it comes to achieving similar success. Perhaps your idea of success is owning a big house, driving a nice car, and having lots of free time to enjoy your life, not only should you look for people who have already achieved those goals, but you should also seek out people who *enjoy* their lives – that's *the key*. For me, success has never been measured simply by numbers in my bank account, but rather by the number of lives I can impact. To properly impact as many as I want, I *have* to be financially capable, but in recent years I've largely been drawn to mentors whose hearts are larger than their sizable financial victories.

I remember meeting a master at network marketing. She earned millions of dollars a year with an upstart multi-level marketing company and was an absolute expert at what she did. I would recommend her skills to anyone interested in achieving wealth within a network marketing world. By appearance, people would assume she had it all, every success. Except for one problem, one large snag that stuck out to me – she worked too hard. It was obvious her health and family life were failing as a result, a glaringly negative result of her labors, at that. It wasn't uncommon for her to work 70, 80, or even 100 hours a week. Yes, it was good money, but at what cost? I would rather learn from a person who knows how to earn money without giving up their families, without giving up their health. Simply put, because I want to be inspired. I want to be inspired to spend time bettering myself. I want to inspire the world around me. And, I want to do it without losing what makes it all worth it in the process.

In the year that our company began to grow, I worked to correct the pains I created in my own family. For too long, I would spend my days on the field training. Arriving before sunrise, I'd soon find myself at home long after sunset and our children's bedtime. The sixteen-hour workday consumed by fulfilling the needs of everyone except for my wife and kids. Now, as our staff has grown, I unapologetically focus on them each morning until their needs are met. Until I have connected with each one *on purpose*. I know my team has the needs of the office contained. I know I can never get this time back with my family, and I so deeply miss all of the time that was lost. This is why I work so hard to find mentors who I can respect in every area of their lives.

Listening to Your Mentors

A particularly shrewd piece of advice once came to me in a fairly humorous way – at least the way it played out was, because I won't soon forget it.

"Listen, Eric, you really need to join EO," a mentor of mine said one day, as he turned towards me in his chair.

"What's EO?" I looked back at him, puzzled.

With fixed eyes he stared right back at me and announced, "It's the single most important thing that's grown my business."

So, I said, "Ok, how do I join EO?"

Without hesitating I applied for membership. Naturally, at my first meeting I was asked why I had joined the organization, being the unique entity that it is. My response? I simply said, "Because my mentor told me to…. by the way…. what *is* EO?" I had a chuckle, and so did some others in the room. But it was true – I didn't have a clue what I'd just joined. I trusted my mentor to lead me in the right direction, so I did very little research on the topic. In the end, I was extremely glad I joined EO. It didn't matter that I appeared unprepared to any of the other members, what mattered was that I'd let the right person into my life, someone who cared about my progress as much as they did my well-being.

EO stands for the Entrepreneurs Organization, it is a network of professionals who work together and support each other. EO's mission is for entrepreneurs to learn and grow into the best possible leaders and people that they can be. There are certain thresholds you have to achieve before you can join, but once in, the membership is priceless – it has definitely been incredible for myself. In fact, it has steadily become a powerful mentorship group of fellow entrepreneurs who deeply believe in each other as well as what they do to make the world a better place.

Shared Experiences Over Advice

For me, the most powerful (and challenging) facet of EO is called "forum." It's a small group of peers, usually consisting of six to ten individuals where, under complete confidentiality, you share the five percent of your life that you share with no one else. Your personal, professional, and family highs and lows. We share in each other's triumphs and frustrations. When you share, unlike most other places in life, if you're looking for advice, you *won't* get it. Instead, the philosophy is to not share advice, but only experiences. For example,, if you're having a relationship issue, someone in the group can share what they've experienced in their relationships. The catch is, however, their experience may or may not help you find a path to the solution of your problem.

The thinking is that by giving advice, you're not giving the person enough credit to come up with solutions of their own. You're not believing they're *smart* enough. Instead, by sharing your experience, or the experience of someone you're close to, you're allowing the person to gather their own information, to make their own decisions based on what they know personally from their own experiences, along with what they now know from you and the others who have shared their stories.

Look at Your Surroundings

Who do you surround yourself with? Are they supportive? Do they call you on your mistakes? Do they hold you accountable for your dreams and fears? Do they share your core values and beliefs? Are they lifting you up instead of pulling your down?

I often think about one individual I hired – someone I've known since they were a child. They'd struggled through the family issues most of us grow through as we become adults, and had bounced around from job to job, surrounded by negativity within their workplaces, and outside of them. Since joining us at Aviator, I witnessed a core change take place within them, and it was greatly because of who they were surrounding themselves with. They went from having only a few uplifting individuals in their life to an A-list of life mentors who are literally, and figuratively, teaching them to fly. I saw their outlook go from deeply negative to endlessly positive, and watched their future open up to things they might never have thought possible.

The same in my life holds true. There have been times when I've fallen in with the wrong crowd. And, whenever that happened, my vision and optimism shifted massively. When I'm not hanging around the right people – people who constantly force me to think bigger, urging me to be better – I always fall apart. Positive people pull you up, hauling you along on their adventure. This momentum becomes critical when you seek out opportunities to make life changes and shifts, especially when your desired conclusion is to become a better, more fulfilled, more loving person. While reading Sir Richard Branson's autobiography *Finding My Virginity*, I was struck by a story he shared regarding registering his new space tourism business with the British government, Virgin Galactic. He stated that "While he was at it" he registered a secondary corporation: Virgin *Inter*galactic as well… just to ensure he wasn't thinking too small. People like Sir Richard constantly inspire me to believe in *more*. To never stop pushing and to never allow my childlike hope and glee to be contained.

There will always be people who come into your life that suck positive energy away from you. They demand to be taken care of. They seem to always have some kind of drama, trauma, or mishap that is "someone else's" fault. These people rarely have overtly bad intentions, but you have to find ways to distance and protect yourself from their negative energy. It's a decision of whether or not you can afford to be drawn down, and whether or not you can afford to *not* have forward momentum to take care of yourself. I am a huge believer in helping those in need, but for some their reliance upon others supersedes their ability to help themselves. Often the only way forward for them is to not be enabled by those who care about their well-being. Over and over in my life I have seen clear patterns of helping too much. The only way to real victory over life is to learn the defining differences between those you can save, and those that must save themselves.

"Try new things, step out of your comfort zone, take risks, do things in ways you've never done them before, ask for help, surround yourself with self-actualized people, become obsessed with the fact that you have one go-round on this planet as the you that is you, and realize how precious and important it is not to squander that."

Jen Sincero

"Surround yourself with only people who are going to life you higher."

Oprah Winfrey

"Surround yourself with people who are smarter than you."

Russell Summons

Chapter 6

Surrounding Yourself With The Right People

None of us live in a box – we don't walk around this planet isolated in a capsule, not affecting, or being affected by those around us. You become a piece of everyone you surround yourself with. So, if you surround yourself with people who are negative and drag you down – who don't believe in themselves and constantly have self-doubt – you're going to feel all of those things, too.

It is critical to really draw yourself into the idea of surrounding yourself with people who are what you want to *become*. All you have to do is start with what you have, and then build from there. Begin by pinpointing your limitations. Sometimes they're emotional or spiritual. Sometimes your limitations are physical (or at least you think they are). Now consider this: the people who have the potential to lift you up often aren't going to look the way you imagined. If you feel like you physically can't do something, who's to say the person who can help you achieve your goals hasn't already overcome the same pain you have? They have the ability to show you that you can actually succeed, despite a perceived physical shortcoming. More often than not we conjure up near-fictional superheroes in our minds when we need help, but I've found that the real superheroes are the people who have shared in the same types of struggles we have.

I think of a man by the name of Nick Santonastasso, who I was fortunate to meet at an EO event. He was carrying a stack of books so high he couldn't see past them from his wheelchair. My wife and I spotted him loading these boxes at the entrance to the venue and I immediately offered to help him carry his things back to the flooded event space. Nick is the bestselling author of *Victim to Victor: How to Overcome the Victim Mentality to Live the Life You Love*. That night, my wife and I invited Nick to dinner, and chatted about life. His story is fascinating, to say the least.

Nick Santonastasso

Born with Hanhart syndrome, this birth defect left him with no legs, no right arm, and a left arm with only one finger. His father tells the story of placing two-year-old Nick on the living room floor while he went to the garage for short moment. Within less than a minute, he heard some strange noises coming from the house. Low and behold, Nick had pushed his toy wagon next to a table, climbed into the wagon, got himself onto a chair, and finally pulled himself up onto the table. As Nick's dad walked back into the room, he let out a swift, excited "What the heck is going on?" Shocked at the site of his son not just sitting on the table – *but dancing to MTV videos.*

Nick hasn't stopped since; wrestling on his high school team, skateboarding, singing and playing music, and ultimately becoming an inspiration to all those around him. In an interview he gave when he was just twelve years old, Nick shared his perception on things, especially how he sees things that look like fun. His end resolve was, basically – and enthusiastically – that he wanted to do them. He wanted to experience the things that were bringing others excitement, happiness even. At one point, the PowerPoint showed him laying on his skateboard, racing down the street, and fearlessly going into a handstand – giddily admitting that he loves to skateboard because he feels like he's flying. Naturally, it's been my hope to share paramotoring with him since I heard his story.

Can you imagine what Nick's life would have been like if his parents told him, "No, you can't do that – you're disabled?" What if his teachers, wrestling coach, band leader, friends, and family members just felt sorry for Nick, and wheeled him around in a confining chair just so he wouldn't "hurt himself" – or face failure on his own terms?

Of course, Nick's personal energy would never have allowed that, just like the two-year-old boy who wouldn't allow himself to be left on the floor when he wanted to dance on the table. He self-identified as a victor, versus a victim, long before he had the words. But, if he had been surrounded by negativity, or people who live in fear, that fearlessness he possesses may very well have been crushed, and Nick would not be the happy, fulfilled, inspirational person he is today.

Nick has become the kind of person people are drawn to; he's positive, empathetic, a warrior physically and emotionally. The people who surround Nick are looking to become like him – not literally, of course – but in a way where they recognize how few the limitations actually are in their own lives. It helps them see just how *attainable* their dreams actually are. By surrounding yourself with people like Nick; people who see the upside in everything, people who take risks, and people who are "living the dream," you will be nothing short of blown away by their positive energy. And, if you're willing, you will become more like them.

Life is Not a Passive Exercise

It's not a matter of osmosis – you can't become like someone better than you just by reading their book or hanging out with them. It takes work. Hard work. And good people will cheer you on the whole way, looking at you with pride, not with jealousy or lament. They will inspire you, push you, motivate you, and show you what life is meant to be.

If you purposely set yourself on a mission to surround yourself with interesting, uplifting people, they will want to be around you, too. You'll quickly become an inspiration and seen as someone "living the good life." Your circle of friends will be an influence on you, and you on them. This puts you in a healthy place – on all levels – physical, emotional, and spiritual.

When we're in that healthy place, we have the energy to serve those around us, so we won't feel the need for outside stimulation. When we're in an unhealthy place, we all naturally revert to "escape mode." Maybe drinking too much, or binge eating. Maybe you start abusing yourself or those around you. If you find yourself in an unhealthy state, trying to escape, surrounding yourself with those who are in a healthy frame of mind, body, and spirit makes all the difference in the world. It makes the biggest difference in your outcome – of who you are meant to be.

I've made it my life's work to be surrounded by incredible people. To find mentors who encourage and inspire me – employees and friends who challenge me, who encourage growth, and family who constantly test my ability to be the best man I can be.

I challenge you to think of the people in your life who bring you up, who better you. Then I challenge you to think of those who do the opposite. Identify the ones who drag you down, add layers of exhaustion behind your eyes, and stress to your soul. Think of who you need to kindly step away from and promise yourself to hold true to it. Even more importantly, choose a few of those positive people we've talked about above – those people who have been in the same shoes you currently wear. Confront your fears and intentionally connect with them. Tell them of your mission to better yourself, tell them of your mission to become *more*. Ask them to share their time, and in turn ask them how you can bless their lives.

You will constantly be amazed by how deeply your inspirations *want* to bless your life… Even if they don't know you yet. Your vulnerability and intention may well inspire those you look up to. It may be the catalyst they need to find ways of working harder in order to give back more, and to grow themselves in a whole new way.

*"A person who never made a mistake
never tried anything new"*

Albert Einstein

*"You must accept that you might fail; then, if you do
your best and still don't win, at least you can be
satisfied that you've tried. If you don't accept failure
as a possibility, you don't set high goals, you don't
branch out, you don't try - you don't take the risk."*

Rosalynn Carter

*"Failure is the key to success each
mistake teaches us something"*

Morihei Ueshiba

Chapter 7

Fail Fast - Question Success

Whenever I'm celebrating an achievement, feeling good about overcoming some obstacle, or patting myself on the back, I force myself to stop. I've found it crucial to my success to take the time to question each victory. Did I succeed because I did something right, or was it just a fluke? Did I succeed because I strategized and planned, or did something just fall into my lap?

By questioning success, we learn so much about what it takes to consistently achieve each victory. We often only scrutinize our failures, rather than our successes, but it's this type of examination that leads to the continual victories we crave. They become intentional, more deserved, and remove the guesswork of whether or not the success came by chance. Instead of questioning failures, celebrating the early knowledge of them and move beyond each, as quickly as you can.

We made a notable mistake in our company once. We placed our bets, invested lots of time, money, and energy into engineering, marketing, and selling an electronic fuel injection adaptation for our most popular engine – the first "EFI" of its kind in the powered paraglider industry. Lots of time and resources went into this project, because we were counting on making it back when the engine manufacturer would (we hoped) accept and purchase our idea. Our EFI had the potential to change the sport for the better, making pilots safer, reducing our carbon footprint, and ensuring more happy Aviators in the process.

Sadly though, it didn't go as well as we'd planned. The engine manufacturer turned us down. We had made a huge investment, and I had to make a decision – "What now?" was the overarching question. Should we try to continue to sell this unit? If so, we'd have to make *another* massive investment to get the margins we needed. Or, should we offer it back to the engineer behind it and say, "Here you go, thank you for all you have done – it's yours?"

We ended up giving the project back to the engineer rather than throw more money at it. He would sell it to his own dealers and keep the dream alive, but we couldn't put Aviator at risk despite how much we believed in pushing our sport forward. The decision hurt at first because we could have sold the units to individuals, and made some decent money off them. But, we realized the ultimate costs down the road would probably exceed our resources, and it was more important to stay true to our core purpose of training as many people as we could, as safely as we'd made possible. We had to remain centrically focused on changing new lives through flight and seeing the world become a better place because of it. The ancillary additions and changes for the sport could come later, after everything else was moving as we believed it should be – toward a better world through our student's experiences.

Moving On

We made the decision to fail quickly; I still feel like we didn't make a mistake, but we swung hard and missed the ball. So, we swept up the debris, and moved on. Even when it hurts, it's better than throwing money, energy, and time after a bad decision. This happens all the time, whether it's making a mistake, dating the wrong person, taking a job you don't like, or buying a lemon of a used car. People are often afraid to admit they made a mistake, so they stay in a place where the original mistake they made compounds, and eventually overtakes their life.

"I've made billions of dollars of failures at Amazon. Literally," Jeff Bezos once said. *"What really matters is that*

companies that don't continue to experiment – companies that don't embrace failure – they eventually get into a desperate position, where the only thing they can do is make a 'Hail Mary' bet at the very end of their corporate existence. I don't believe in bet-the-company bets." The same is true in life – if we are willing to make mistakes, learn from them, and develop the ability to move forward with our heads held high, there's not much that can stop us.

Early in my twenties, I lost nearly every cent to my name... in twenty minutes. When the market crashed in 2008, I had made some extremely profitable investments in international currency. As things started to go downhill, I remember sitting in front of my computer screen, watching it all disappear, literally, before my eyes. At a certain point, I lit a cigar, and watched as the number turned to a big fat zero. But, it was ok. I knew there was another day. I was young, I had the energy and hustle to rebuild. I knew that behind every failure lies another opportunity.

The Five-Year Rule

"If in five years, it won't matter, don't waste away the moments of the now, holding onto the worries of 'what if.'"

As I watched my money tick away, I refused to allow myself to grovel, to hold onto a situation which was doomed – I literally, and figuratively, had to let it go. I knew, in five years, this incident wouldn't affect me. Indeed, five years later my circumstances were completely different, and the lost money had found its way back. By letting go, I was able to move on to bigger and better things.

Many people are afraid to let things go. I see it most often in relationships; I see people who are together far longer than they should be – both parties hurting each other. There's so much built-up pain the relationship is never going to be good. I grew up in a conservative family where divorce was never considered an option – it wasn't something you did. Ever. But sometimes removal *is* the best solution. Whether you are divorcing a person, a business, a decision, or a project, being willing to focus on what makes your life best and allows you to build toward a greater goal is key. Holding on to losing cards with the full knowledge there is no way out *through* them is not living at all. It is simply refusing to let go.

When you live your life in a way that is not fulfilling, or in a way that does not bring joy to you, you are unable to bring joy to someone else's life. On the surface, it may seem selfish to put your needs over others', but your needs are critical to happiness and experiencing fulfilment. When you are living a full life, it's easy for you to give back to those you love, and those who need a hand-up. Taking care of yourself is absolutely necessary when it comes to taking care of others.

If we are put on this earth, for no other reason, but to live the life we have, what is it supposed to look like? What are our decisions supposed to look like?

I believe we need to make sure that everything we do here, today, while we are alive in our bodies, amplifies other peoples' lives. We need to ensure we're doing everything we can to live our best life – for ourselves, for our children, for our family, for our friends, for our colleagues, and for the world in general. If you were to remove the filter of the possibility of an afterlife, and say we are only here for this time on earth, what would it look like? Or rather, what *should* it look like?

For some people that might look like going to church every Sunday and volunteering in their community. Or it may look like donating money to charity. For others it may look like spending every possible moment they can with their children. Still for others it might look like believing in themselves and being adventurous. At the end of the day, we are meant to ensure we are bettering the world, living in a healthy place, willing to let go of our failures and grow on, through them.

Meeting Who You're Supposed to Be

Entrepreneur, Ed Myllet, has an interesting take on this. He often shares that when he dies, he expects to go to heaven and meet the person he was supposed to be. We all have our perspectives on what an afterlife will, or will not, consist of. Though I grew up in a conservative Christian home, I don't claim to know what the absolute truth is. I constantly research and analyze every possibility I can. I've often thought that if reincarnation is real, then living on earth, at any given time, can be considered heaven *and* hell at the same time; it's our choice of how we want to live *now*, in either heaven or hell. We make the decision ourselves whether our time on earth will be a living hell or a living heaven.

We do this by learning from our mistakes, not holding them in our victim bag. By living our lives in a way where we have the energy, happiness, and fulfillment we need we can better the lives of those around us.

It took me fifteen years after becoming eligible to actually *get* my pilot's license. I had over 1,200 hours of flight time in fixed-wing ultralights and aircraft, had been signed off to fly dozens of types of aircraft, but I found comfort in not stretching myself enough. I had a multitude of pilots who would sign me off on flying any myriad of planes, and go pretty much anywhere I wanted to go, as long as I didn't have a passenger. So, I could fly by myself all the time. It wasn't until I had children that I was finally willing to do the thing that scared me the most – taking the written test.

I was homeschooled, and never took standardized tests. I didn't know how to study for them and wasn't even sure how to begin, not even for the FAA's Private Pilot exam, which focused on my specialty – Aviation. But then, my children started asking me, "Daddy, when are you going to take me flying?"

This was the beginning of the push I needed, so I shared it with my wife one night – "Ok, I'm going to do it," I said.

That same week, it so happened, my cousin was going in to take his written test. He had come over for dinner, and casually mentioned, "I'm taking my written exam in a couple days."

I immediately spotted the rest of the encouragement I needed… "Can I take it with you?" I asked.

"Um, yeah, sure!" he replied, and also unwittingly became my mentor for it in the process.

I had two days to prepare and I was absolutely terrified of failing the test. Stressing, until I finally realized that if I failed the test, at least I tried. *I've put it off for fifteen years. What could I lose by taking the test and failing it?* I reasoned within myself. From there I put away my feelings of inadequacy, maybe I didn't have it in me to succeed, but by God, I had to try.

With just two days to cram – two days to study, understand, and remember everything I had to know in order to pass so I could fly with my children – I walked into the testing room stone-cold terrified.

But, I passed.

Overcoming

I felt giddy. But also *so* silly. I had built up that single fear for so long, not believing in myself, and not being willing to take a simple risk. I wasn't willing to put in the hard work. Sure, it was only two days, but two days is a long time to take away from family and business and everything else important in my life. I was putting something off I *needed* – something that proved to make me a better person, and would make me proud of myself – so I could better serve those around me. My children could fly with me. I could share my love of flying with others in a whole new way. Why hadn't I faced my fear? What was it that overwhelmed me?

I'm not wholly sure, really. But my lesson was clear. To embrace success, we must question it to better understand the why, to welcome and learn from failure, and then overcome it. I had failed myself by waiting so long, but ultimately a few days after passing my checkride, I was able to take my first passenger, my wife, to lunch. Flying her a few cities away in a fraction of the time it would have taken us to drive. It was a simple flight, one I'd made many times before, alone. But I shed a tear that day. Not out of lament for waiting so long, but out of the joy of finally sharing something I love with someone I love. Those joyful tears were shed for overcoming my failure.

My friend, the father who lost his daughter, became something bigger than himself *because* of his loss. He shared with me how, prior to learning to fly and becoming a part of our flying family, he had done *nothing* for himself since she had left them. He was too busy taking care of everyone around him; protecting them and making sure they were alright. It was out of obligation, of course, and out of love, clearly; but it was also drawn from the part of himself that didn't want to take the time to look at the grief in the eyes. He was hiding from his pain, afraid to face the man it may have made him.

Once he did, however, he became a bigger, better, and far more fulfilled and open person for it. His heart grew to the point that he then wanted to touch lives less fortunate, to help others who might be grieving too. So, I told him about my idea to start a foundation that would bring the joy of flying to those who can't afford it, to veterans who are recovering from PTSD, to impoverished school children in the inner city who have never flown before, and most importantly, working to defend our liberty of flight from public airports in the US. He was overjoyed by the idea… and together, we've been doing that work ever since.

"A leader is one who knows the way, shows the way and goes the way."

John C. Maxwell

"The secret to success is good leadership, and good leadership is all about making the lives of your team members or workers better."

Tony Dungy

"The growth and development of people is the highest calling of leadership."

Harvey Firestone

Chapter 8

Leadership Within the Team

Back in the 1980s, a young, inexperienced manager named Jack Stack took over the Springfield Remanufacturing Corporation, an almost bankrupt division of International Harvester. He didn't really know how to manage a company, but he had experience on the playing field and understood the principles of athletic competition and the basics of democracy. From there, he created his own style of management called, "Open-Book Management."

With this philosophy, Stack insisted on making sure everyone in the organization had a say on financial decisions. All the books, including executive pay, expense accounts, supply costs, and tax expenses, were made available to all employees. In fact, everyone at Springfield learned how to read a profit and loss statement. Employees had a say in operations, short- and long-term strategy, and voted in company matters.

In his classic book, *The Great Game of Business*, first published more than 20 years ago, Stack shares this strategy and how he was able to turn the fate of Springfield Manufacturing Corporation around. He remained as president and CEO in the now employee-owned business. His philosophy hasn't been widely adopted, but I saw something in there I knew would help me and Aviator.

I texted my dad, who has also been a lifelong entrepreneur, and told him we were going to do this "open-book" concept. He called me, his words dripping with horror, "Eric, you can't do that! You're crazy!" But when he finally read the book for himself, he not only liked it, but he agreed it could transform everything we were doing.

Scaling Up in Business and Life

When we decided to scale-up our business, to move from a "hobby" business to a power in the community – and beyond – it didn't happen easily. As I shared earlier, I lost a valued business partner due to the change, as well as our well-loved, long-time employees. It was tricky to navigate the change from a small-time business, to one with a greater vision. We'd been plagued for years with emails, phone calls, and posts from wonderful folks who wanted to join us in the skies. They'd absorbed our videos, seen how our Aviator syllabus looked and the results it produced, and then opted for a more local school, expecting the same results and the same familial experience. It was always a struggle to read those messages because the other schools marketed themselves as if they offered the same level of service, of family, that we do, but their priorities are certainly different. One critical email forced me to open my eyes and realize we had to grow. Unsettled, I read that a couple invested over $30,000 in their gear and training with another company. They'd taken a week off of work, and had walked away with a terrible taste in their mouth. Barely any training had been completed, they had no confidence, and zero flights. Their experience *could* have been life changing and positive. A husband and wife stepping forward together to do something transformational. Instead, they were disgusted, upset, and felt like they'd wasted not just money, but time.

It was emails like this that convinced me to move forward. We couldn't carry on as a small company, satisfied with helping the few we were able to at our size. We had a *moral obligation* to learn how to serve more people, and to help them experience the transformational change in themselves that I'd personally experienced: overcoming fear through flight. Doing something *superhuman.*

So, we opened our books and shared our plan with our team on December 1, 2018. And since that date, our business has grown exponentially – again, not without some hardship. As I mentioned above, we lost 100 percent of our original employees, everyone gone, except for me. Everyone got off the bus, as their roles became more defined. They all decided it wasn't right for them, and this new mission wasn't a good fit for their lives. On one hand, it terrified me, but I *knew* we were on the right track. We *had* to grow in order to serve our clients properly. In order to fulfill the mission of changing lives we had set before us.

The people who have filled our positions since then are beyond incredible, they are the *right* people. They are not just growing our business, but they believe in what we're trying to do. They see the vision. They see we want to change people's lives through flight. They *own* that vision of what we're trying to do and they're willing to do the work that's needed to achieve our mission.

We use a hybrid of the EOS (Entrepreneurial Operating System) and the Gazelles' "Scaling Up" processes to ensure we have sound systems in place. Within two weeks of hiring, our plug-and-play systems are designed to train a new employee to know exactly what to do, and what's expected of them. The entire system of management ensuring we can make the hard decisions necessary to build a business; to be willing to take the required risks and to be confident the outcome will be positive.

The Risks of Change

I was concerned we might lose employees when we shared our new vision for where we were going. Though, I never would have guessed we would lose *everyone,* much less my business partner, to this expanded vision and more accurate focus. But, everyone that departed left amicably and it's *all* been worth it. We are changing more lives, saving them from having negative experiences associated with their dreams of flight. We are doing what we are *meant* to do.

It takes a lot of belief in what you're doing to push this hard, to accept the surprises and changes. If you don't have a higher purpose in your business, in your life, it would be almost impossible to survive change like this. If you're just existing, staying afloat, you're never going to hit the level you *need* to be at. Through these changes, we shifted our mission from being a great place to learn how to fly, to a great place to learn how to become a better person.

Gurus like Tony Robbins do this by having people walk on coals. We do it by strapping motors on people's backs and helping them run into the sky.

Below the surface – what people don't know – is that in the fall of 2018, the same time we made the decision to implement this immense change in our business model (which catapulted our business), we were actually considering selling out and giving the business up to the highest bidder. That is, as long as they were a past student who understood what we did, and why. We were so exhausted from working *in* the business, instead of working *on* the business, that we met with two of our mentors and past students. Men I deeply respect, intending to sell the business to one, or both of them.

Instead, through two days of deep, insightful conversation, we walked away with the intention of massively growing the business in our perspective, our operations, and our mission. When great employees and friends leave because they can't stay on the bus for their own good, it's hard. But we've remained on good terms despite the hardship, and we all realize we appreciate each other for following our own paths.

Once you make a decision to push, to grow, and to change you will have people who simply can't keep up. It's not because they're bad people, it's because it doesn't fit their culture. Two years ago, we were sitting around our schoolhouse, flying mini FPV drones around, laughing, and playing because we didn't have any more work to be accomplished for the day. Now, there's a new, clear goal everyone strives for – every day. We moved from a mom-and-pop hobby business mentality into a company that has bigger goals, service tickets, more complex processes, and a desire to serve more people, all while they see their dreams becoming reality. This all started in my first home's garage.

Sometimes when I think of how far we've come I'm simply blown away.

Changing Your Life

Sometimes this sort of thing spills over into your personal life. As business changes from a hobby to a more serious goal, priorities shift. A big part of the reason we chose to change the business model wasn't just the knowledge that we were promoting our beloved sport, inspiring people to join it, and then not having the availability to serve them, it was because, for the seven years of my children's lives – those seven years spent working on Aviator – there were often four, five, even seven days in a row where I hadn't seen them at all. I might've slept in the same house, but I would head out to work before they woke up and get home long after they fell asleep. It became a huge weight on my shoulders. I felt like I didn't even know them, like I wasn't doing my part to support my family in a physical, emotional, or spiritual capacity. I felt like I was abandoning my wife to the hard work of raising them, and the blessed parts of enjoying their company.

By choosing to grow and give up parts of the business to people who are more capable of handling it, I no longer have to be in the field every day. I don't have to be the one talking people up for their first flights. Although I'll always miss those joys, those experiences, it's still so worth it to be able to see my daughter and two sons every morning. It's worth it to see them as they change and grow. For me, it's never been about making a trillion dollars in any business, but creating a safe environment where my family can be comfortably confident so we can share experiences and adventures. I want us to be able to *truly* experience the world around us.

Strength in Vulnerability

The number one leadership quality I most value is vulnerability. Only through the ability to be genuinely open and honest – with yourself and your employees – is the foundation of a strong team laid. When I'm struggling with something at home, or when I'm having a day where I'm really struggling with the death of my brother, I'm not afraid to share my pain, my frustration, my sadness. In fact, I welcome the opportunity to open my heart and express who I *truly* am. I've seen it empower my team to know and see that we *all* struggle. Without sharing the challenges we experience, we isolate ourselves and we're left alone, seemingly strong, but hopelessly unable to overcome. By choosing to be open together we learn to triumph over life's hardships… together.

At Aviator, we are always looking for people who are servants *first*, who exemplify openness and vulnerability, who think big, and are willing to constantly choose joy.

Optimism, and real integrity, is what I believe defines the greatest leaders in any team. Anyone can point out problems, but it takes an *optimist* to find a solution; and a wholesome person to recognize when there may be a better member of the team to fulfill the need.

"Setting goals is the first step in turning the invisible into the visible."

Tony Robbins

"What you get by achieving your goals is not as important as what you become by achieving your goals."

Zig Ziglar

"Set your goals high and don't stop until you get there."

Bo Jackson

Chapter 9

The Necessity to Have BIG Goals

People who lead unsatisfied, depressed lives, struggling through it all, may sometimes be in the middle of overcoming overwhelming hardship. But, often that's not the case. More frequently, I've found they are struggling because they have trained themselves (or been trained) to not think big *enough*. They struggle because they don't have enough gumption or belief in themselves to know in their hearts that they can do something truly great, even world changing.

I've had friendships (which quickly fell apart) where my counterpart didn't have a dream. Sometimes, they didn't know how to dream or the *natural* ability to do so had been torn away from them by some trauma in their life they were constantly living with. They sometimes fought through everyday facets of life or struggled with depression. In my own history, I have not been so different from them… I get down, I worry, I struggle. Until I move the finish line forward or back and take on something else. Until I replace my failed goal with something else that matters to me. Until I believe I can, will, and *must* achieve another big step forward for my life.

I have always tried to find things in life that motivate my soul, whether it's a monetary goal or to see students join us and succeed themselves. My goals have included sales goals, the number of hours flown by our students, a certain number of hours spent personally in the air each week, or time spent focused on my wife and children. They can be a personal challenge like running a marathon, spending ten days adventuring with my children each year, or finding a new way to show my wife I love her… and knowing she truly feels it.

Goals are often set with numbers, but the numbers are just a guide, the goals themselves are about so much more. They're in the hearts of our employees, our families, and our friends. If we set a goal at Aviator to do 2,000 additional flights with students this year, we know very well it may mean we'll miss a lot of mornings with our children or loved ones. So, I encourage everyone on our team to focus and ensure they spend more *intentional* time with them when they can, instead of playing on our phones or getting distracted by other frivolous things. To not disengage, but truly be present and ensure that those we love *know* we care and are fully signed on to our future sacrifice.

Money is a scorecard for me, it's important, yes. But it's not the end result. If I were to make a trillion dollars in a year, but didn't spend quality time with my family building memories and ensuring our mutual strength… or give myself time to pursue the things I love, what's the point? Sure, money enables us to do more for more people. It enables us to have confidence and security. But, it's not the end all, be all. It's *never* been my end goal.

I have a different perspective on goals, actually. Since I was a child I've constantly given myself little incentives that motivated me to reach my target. When I was a kid, I found ways to reward myself for even the most mundane of tasks. As a homeschooled child, it was freeing myself to read a chapter of whatever biography I was excited about after completing every page of math. As a teen, it was freeing myself to go flying every morning after completing my required chores and homework. Today, anytime I hit a personal goal, or point of success, whether it's getting my pilot's license or growing the business past a certain point of revenue, I buy myself a watch. Or if I'm lucky, sometimes an airplane. I work to constantly level up my life and my impression of it. To some it may seem petty from the outside, but for my heart, it's invaluable.

My obsession with watches came from an unlikely source: comedian, Kevin Hart. One day, rewarding myself for finally completing a difficult project, I spent some time watching interviews of interesting people on YouTube. I went down the rabbit hole of related videos until I found myself engaged with funny guy Kevin sharing his fascination with watches. He spoke passionately about how he invested in fine timepieces after each project, movie, and tour he completed to symbolize not just the success of the project, but more importantly, to symbolize the time he'd spent away from those who mattered most to him. Time he would never get back. Today, I encourage all of my family and our team at Aviator to deeply value their time, to find things that both inspire and enable them to strive toward their personal goals.

When my brother James passed, I spent months deep diving eBay, Chrono24, and other websites, combing them for watches made in 1995, the year he was born. When I finally found one I felt matched the personalities and style of every member of our family, I unveiled them at Christmas. Something for each of us to remember our time with him.

Reward Yourself

Having something out there you can hold onto as a future reward is an incredible incentive to not just complete your goals, but to propel yourself well beyond them.

When I was a child, my parents had a sticky note on their bathroom mirror with a list of their goals – a list of things they wanted to accomplish that year. I remember seeing it and thinking it didn't make much sense. I thought writing down your goals was silly until I started living it myself.

Since my teens, I'd always wanted to buy a Piper Cub, a plane built in the 1940s. I learned to fly in one, registration number NC6666H (yes, it had that many sixes in it). You've probably seen a Cub. They're the ubiquitous antique, yellow, single engine airplane, with chunky little tires and a single propeller that has to be pulled through by hand to start. I fell in love with flying partly because of that beautiful, yellow airplane, and it was always my dream to have one of my own so I could use it to help young people just like I had been helped by my flying mentor. They shared their aircraft with me, so I could learn (and love) to fly. I *needed* to do that for others. The hunt for a Piper Cub was the perfect incentive for me to avidly meet my goal of helping others and fulfil a dream set in my youth.

Symbols of Success

One day, a student turned friend brought in a massive commemorative coin stamped by Piper with the image of the Cub on its side. He knew of my love for the plane, and I was beyond appreciative of that little trinket. However, something pretty spectacular happened after he gave it to me. It laser focused my childhood dream. I put it on my desk and stared at it every day – I saw it as a symbol of success, of what I wanted to do. For months, looking at that coin became a motivation for me to reach my goal of owning a Cub. And, of being able to serve others like I myself had been served.

It wasn't until one day, after months of shopping around, when another friend gave me a call. I was walking with my family along the shores of Lake Wailes, enjoying live music, fresh meals from food trucks, and lots of laughter. "I found your Cub!" he exclaimed. I immediately stood still amidst the festivities, motioning for Nelle to come closer. We'd just sold our first home and had some equity built up – *it was time* – so with my wife's encouragement, I bought it on the spot. Going to inspect and pick it up the very next day was my reward coming to fruition – on so many levels. Not only did it fulfill my childhood dream of owning a Piper Cub, but it was also a reward for achieving a place of comfort financially that my wife and I had worked very hard for. Yet it was an even bigger reward in what it meant for making my underlying dream a reality – I could now use the aircraft to inspire others. It opened a new way I could instill a love for flight.

Set a goal. Make it a big one… and when you achieve it, be willing to reward yourself. Within moments of agreeing to buy my Cub, I felt a twinge of buyer's remorse, worrying that treating myself to something I so deeply wanted wasn't the wisest use of our capital. Luckily, my wife was there to remind me that I *needed* to relish in my victories, I needed to meet my goals, and without investing in my own happiness, none of the work is truly worth it. She was clear in pointing out that by purchasing the plane I was actually moving myself forward, closer to where I wanted to be in life.

My friend Trent Palmer made an incredible video he shared with the world (its titled "THIS is what it's all about," look it up on YouTube!). In it, he shares his profound thoughts:

"It's moments like these, days like these, that make me realize what life is all about. It's not about making money, you can always make more of that, or having cool toys... because if you don't make time to enjoy them, then what's the point?

It's about USING the time you have here, in this life, to its full potential. Enjoying the playground that is the world we live in, alongside the company of good friends.

It's too easy to get carried away with the obligations and the grind of life. To get stuck in the groove of work, eat, sleep, repeat. Endlessly searching for the point where you can retire, relax, and finally enjoy life. More often than not, we work away all the golden years of our lives. Years we will never get back. All in an attempt to enjoy the remaining few.

I say, it doesn't have to be that way. I know we have all seen the motivational posts and heard the uplifting speeches

that tell us to live our fullest life…. But what is it that stops us?
Self-structured limitations. One's often not justified by
anything more than the fear of stepping outside of our comfort
zone. It's these artificial walls that are the true killers here.
The ones that we allow to stop us from living in the moment.
In telling you this, I'm telling you to stop waiting, stop
dreaming, and start LIVING life. Life is too short to eat dessert
last."

I encourage you to read those words, to consider them well. To acknowledge the limitations you've placed on yourself, the barriers that have kept you from living your best life… and to put something new in their place. *Real* goals, with *real* rewards. Perhaps it's coming to learn to fly with us at Aviator, perhaps it's a special trip with your family, or a quiet weekend to refocus yourself on who you are meant to be. Realize *you* have been designed to be bigger than your obstacles and get on to *really* living.

What is your dream and who are you because of it?

As a business owner, I feel it's my responsibility to encourage the same mindset in my team. We set goals and offer our team a reward for achievement. It could feel manipulative if wasn't done with the right purpose. But, if the goals are set *by* the team, and achieved for the greater good, it aligns with our purpose. We've seen it unify and strengthen our company. Sometimes I choose to offer a reward after the fact. An unexpected blessing. My favorite is to bless them with an outing, or a bonus, or some other type of reward outside of any framework of "when we meet this goal, you will get *x*." It changes things from expectations into feelings of genuine gratitude, of feeling appreciated. My favorite thing to do as a CEO is to learn the dreams of my team and to help them realize them. Whether it's more education, a unique experience, or a special time with family. I love to see their joy. Ultimately, if your desire is to see the joy in others, you're giving your employees the opportunity to truly live – even in the workplace.

Set a Metric – What is the Symbol of Your Success?

Not only is setting goals critical, making them *visible* to your daily life is a must. Taking time to know what reward will drive you to accomplish your goal is a must. But how do you actually accomplish the task of meeting your desired results?

Writing down targets or goals, whether it's for your personal life or a business goal, can help you stay focused and make it tangible – something you can see, touch, feel, and measure. Only then can you achieve it.

If you set the *big* goal of being debt free, living in a beautiful home, having two months each year free to travel, and having the funds to sustain you, it may seem like a monster. Like it's too large to overcome. But if you build sustainable goals in between that monster (with the bigger vision still in the back of your mind), your smaller rewards will constantly push you forward.

In Gino Wickman's book, *Leverage,* he talks about creating a ten-year target, a three-year picture, and a one-year plan (I use a five-year target for my personal life and business because it feels more attainable for me). Each week, month, and quarter you revise your short-term goals, reward yourself for those you have completed, and enhance your focus on those you haven't. Insurmountable goals quickly become attainable when broken down. So, take your goals and break them down.

Perhaps first work your way through your high-interest debt; climb the ladder at work until you're in a position with more time off; focus on being present with your family when you're home; "read" a non-fiction, life affirming book through Audible each day on your way to and from work; because each of those is *doable.* If you track each step of the way, your heart will feel immensely more fulfilled as you continue your journey toward the higher goal. Remember, you never know how you're doing unless you *track* it. Write down your successes, cross things off lists, be aware of your journey.

Being clear and concise about your goals helps you share them with others, it also helps you visualize what your life could be for you and those you love. If you're able to see a certain level of success for your coworkers, clients, and employees, you're going to see what you need to provide them with to help them succeed.

Each of my students, each of my employees, has a dream, and I want to help everyone fulfill them. So, how do I do that? Everything has to be measurable. If you're not growing, you're *dying*. If you don't measure whether or not you have growth, you're dying already. And you may not even know it.

Being around people who are living their dream – whether their dream is a fancy car, a big house, or retiring early and enjoying life traveling and adventuring – surrounding yourself with their successes helps you feel like you can touch that dream. It's real. It's not a fantasy. Find people *doing it*, who have achieved the symbol of their success you most value. Being around people who dream as big as you is everything.

Each of us struggle. There is an inner turmoil in everything we do. To some degree, we all have a belief that maybe we're not worthy of success or of meeting our goals. We believe we're not capable, or we're not *enough*. It's normal to have disbelief because we've been told we're not enough for most of our lives. Whether or not we've actually been told that, word for word, by an impatient teacher, our parents, siblings, or supervisors, perhaps we've come to believe it as our reality. As human beings we are hardwired to have extreme doubts about ourselves. Even in our most healthy state emotionally and mentally, we are frequently our greatest critics. Surrounding yourself with those who believe in your vision and *want* to see you succeed is crucial to realizing the success you dream of.

Rejecting "No"

Every time we've been told "no," either by ourselves, or by someone else, we're told we're not *enough*. We have to force ourselves to push beyond this, to believe we *are* enough, that we are worth it. *You* deserve success and happiness. Sometimes, it can feel like a steep uphill climb. There is a point in life, however, when it becomes easier. As one of my mentors, Luke Gifford says, "*You are only as strong as your practices… And you are always practicing.*"

The practice of living purposefully can be hard to comprehend until you break it down beyond the complexities of your world. In late 2019 I was blessed to spend time caring for my children while my wife learned to fly. Within a few days of being home full time I recognized something was missing in their lives. They had school, chores, and responsibilities. They had a schedule, and expectations for behaviors. But they lacked direction toward a *larger* goal. Something bigger than themselves that drew on the parts of them that would define them as they grow up. That larger goal that will help define them as great or help them see where they lack discipline. So, we started working on that. I began sharing a list of things my own heart wanted so as to encourage their young souls to create the same. Then, we started working together to build achievable goals that were aimed at helping them grow beyond the day-to-day. Because they, just like you, deserve a life beyond the monotony of repetition.

You deserve to have a life that is fulfilling. You deserve a life that is challenging, but with challenges you can overcome. You deserve love. You deserve a life of adventure. Each of us have these core things we deserve, but we spend much of our lives questioning and doubting it.

Perhaps the best way to move beyond those doubts is helping others feel *their* value. It can inspire you to feel the same for yourself. Every morning, I make sure I spend real, genuine time with each of my children and my wife, to make sure they feel loved and valued. I do the same when I get to work. I make sure I say hello and high five or hug every single employee at each of our buildings in our hometown, to make sure they know they are an important part of our company… and most crucially, to show how invaluable *they* are to me.

Affirming their importance to me, my vision, and to our team is everything to me. I believe our company culture is defined and ensured by my role as CEO. These incredible people have come alongside me because they believe in what we're doing, but I need to affirm that *I* believe in them too because every day holds its own challenges.

When you're a business owner or work in a small, growing company, nearly every day feels like a Monday. But it's okay when you're surrounded by people you love and value, who in turn value and love you too. Believing in each other gives us a much-needed affirmation. Plus, it's a great way to start the day. No matter what comes up, you know these people have your back, and they know you have theirs.

I even had one of our employees tell me that this was the first job he'd ever had that when five o'clock comes around he gets sad and has no desire to go home. What an awesome goal to have for your employees. To have a place you've create for those who are helping you achieve your life goals, and you theirs.

Work as Your Purpose

One of the things I recognize is that my chosen profession isn't just about teaching people the joys of flight. It really is about encouraging people to be inspired and motivated to see what they can do with their own lives. To show them that, yes, there are limits, but there are much fewer than most of us imagine. The business side of achieving that is great – I love my business. But, at the end of the day, I realize my mission is much grander than just what I do for a living.

What would it be like if a business owner went around to each of their employees and asked them what their dream was? And, then did the same thing with each client: "What's your dream? How can I help you achieve it?" Consider how this could shift the way we think about our businesses, as well as how we go through life.

What is your purpose? What is your higher purpose? Can you help those around you envision theirs? How about your company? What is its purpose? What is its *highest* purpose? Is it something every employee knows and feels to be true? Do you reflect on that as a team? Does everyone know their role and place in achieving that vision?

Lisa Earle McLeod wrote in her book, *Selling With A Noble Purpose*:

"How will your customer be <u>different</u> as a result of doing business with you?"

We constantly ask that question at Aviator. Our whole team lives and breathes service and joy with our goal to encourage every student and client to become the version of themselves they always dreamt they might be.

What's Your Next Goal?

Students come to us so we can help them achieve a major goal in their life. Most of them have always wanted to fly, and by following our systems they can do that. But, then what? Once they've achieved that huge step forward in their life, what's their next goal? What's their next mountain to climb, either literally or figuratively?

We grow by setting new, higher, larger goals that help rejuvenate our souls, mind, and body. Once people have experienced flight, and have become proficient, the last thing we leave them with is that it's not meant to die with them. It's not something designed to just fulfill *them*. How can they give back to the sport, to their loved ones, to their community? Use *giving back* as a basis for your next goal.

Once you've achieved a goal, you will have a deeper well to draw from; whether it's financial, spiritual, or emotional. You have that much more you can give back. You have more depth to your experience and to your life-lessons What will you do with it?

"Happiness consists in giving, and in serving others."

Henry Drummond

"The more generous we are, the more joyous we become. The more cooperative we are, the more valuable we become. The more enthusiastic we are, the more productive we become. The more serving we are, the more prosperous we become."

William Arthur Ward

"The best way to find yourself is to lose yourself in the service of others."

Mahatma Gandhi

Chapter 10

The Importance of Serving Others

I was raised in a family of hard workers. My mom and dad had all of us kids involved in two different businesses; selling books for homeschoolers and the five-star bed and breakfast founded in 1931 by my great-grandmother. These were two businesses where service was everything, and we charged with taking care of everyone who came to us.

My parents' business was different than everyone else's on the market. Their business model was never to sell based on price. Their model was to build customer loyalty based on service, and at a price no higher (or lower) than retail. My mother read every book we sold and wrote a short review for each one. We had a catalog we distributed every year titled, "The Always Incomplete Resource Guide and

Catalog," containing thousands and thousands of reviews each painstakingly written by her delicate hands.

Every weekend, six months of the year, we'd find ourselves in a different city, setting up for a homeschool convention. We would empty the mass of products out of our trailer and set up each of the thousands of titles we'd taken along, fully exhausted by the end of each set up day. Local families would then spend their weekend planning the school year ahead, researching everything they could, and leaning on us for help. My mother would make personal recommendations and hand them to the parents. Most of the time they had deer-in-the-headlights faces, clearly overwhelmed by it all. Mom would sometimes hold their hand and say, "Take them home tonight, look them over, take your time, and make sure you think they will work for you." Dumbfounded, they would look at my mom and say, "But, what if we don't pay for them?" She would smile wryly and say, "Well, for us it's just books, for you it's eternal consequences." We never had anyone *not* return the books in over twenty years of business.

My great-grandmother's bed and breakfast, the Chalet Suzanne, was home to my first job. My initial role was getting the giant vats of pour through coffee brewing each morning so it would be ready for service. At six in the morning I would rise and make the 200-yard commute from our home to the restaurant, starting the first daily batch in the big, stainless steel percolators. To make it "Chalet strong" I'd carefully recirculate the brewed coffee back through the grounds once each side, decaf and regular. My mentors/bosses at the time thinking nothing of a child holding gallons of scalding coffee above his head in order to get the job done. Later I took on many other roles. My grandmother, Vita, was a consummate host; the Chalet was a famous and high-end restaurant with the average bill coming in at over $400 dollars for two (if they enjoyed wine). In the 1960s it became the go-to place for astronauts in the heyday of the program in Florida, since the restaurant was just a fifteen-minute flight away from the chaos of Cocoa Beach in their NASA provided T-38s. One of our most frequent guests was James "Jim" Irwin of Apollo 15 fame. By the time I was born, he'd become like family to all of us. He was like a grandfather to my siblings and I (we called him Opa), and his grandkids to this day are all considered cousins.

Until her health failed in her seventies, my grandmother greeted everyone who came into the restaurant personally. She ensured they had the best possible time, and that they had everything they needed. She engrained in our lives that what we wanted, even what we needed, wasn't nearly as valuable as ensuring the experiences of our guests. Making it not just worthy of their money, but worthy of their time. Nothing was to be left undone and everything needed to be done *perfectly*. Life was about sharing joy, ensuring everyone left happier and more whole than they'd come.

This became such a big part of who I am, it still defines a piece of my core philosophy and most closely held beliefs. It's important to me to be in service to others, and to give, always. I frequently consider others around me and how they choose to serve. I look for others who think the same way, invite them into my life and into the lives of my family. These are the type of people I encourage to join our team… For at the core of all we do, we are here to *serve*.

Team Service

We hire based on our core values. Solely. One of those core values is having a servant's heart. The best members of our team are the ones who are willing to do anything and everything it takes to serve our clients and each other. They naturally recognize they're part of a team. They're happy to pick up a broom, if needed, just like I am. I don't mind twisting a wrench or cleaning the bathroom, and neither do my teammates. These genuine servants don't look at any task as "below" them. They just see what needs to be done and do it.

We share that philosophy with our students through our "five rules," a part of our mantra at Aviator, and as I mentioned before the final rule is to "Give Back." To find something to give back to – your community, your world, even the sport itself. We ask them to find a way to build on that notion of service. This is also why we started our non-profit, the Aviator Foundation. With it, we ensure the opportunity for our fellow pilots to continue to exercise their rights, and we bring aviation, adventure, and passion to people who may not be able to afford it.

We try to *inspire* inspiration – to see how we can bring a bigger joy to the world around us. People with service in their hearts are the types of people I want to be around, because I want to be more and more like them. We create beautiful lives for ourselves and others by serving others, sharing joy and choosing to ensure others around us are blessed. We live a life of gratitude, rather than choosing to be the victim of our circumstances.

Giving Without Expectations

Some people think of this as a type of karma, but I'm not really comfortable with that. With the notion of karma, I think the motivation can sometimes be self-serving. Doing something nice and expecting good "karma" as a result. Instead, if I choose to do something nice, I find that without expectations or even thinking about it, my life improves. You've probably seen it in your own life or in the lives of others who live as natural servants.

Things in life are ancillary. It's the relationships you make and nurture, and the way you build up the lives of those around you that matter most. As much as I appreciate some of the "things" I have, they don't hold a candle to the relationships in my life. It's always about inspiring others to live lives that are more fulfilling, whether they are my children, my wife, my team, our clients, or my neighbors. There is nothing sadder in this world than a wealthy man or woman with a selfish heart.

We see this in our classes. Students come in thinking they just want to learn how to fly, but through the process of bonding by way of a common goal, they leave transformed. From the strait-laced serious engineer transforming into a giddy new pilot, to the stroke victim smiling from ear to ear no longer awkward about his deformities. People start class as one person, and if they let it, the experience changes them powerfully into another. They leave as a renewed, more whole person just two weeks later. That's what our service is about. Yes, they learn how to fly, but they also learn how to be in their own skin, how to see things with new eyes and ears. They are changed, and they are asked to turn right back around and give back so that others can experience what they have.

Generosity of Spirit

I've been blessed in my life. There have been moments my hard work has paid off and my family has had everything they needed to survive, which left me with the opportunity to bless others. Whether it's slipping a few bills into the mailboxes of acquaintances on Christmas Day, over tipping like a madman at my favorite restaurants, or donating to the fundraisers of hurting strangers, I've always felt it's my duty to ensure I not only gave back to those who were in need, but also to help my children understand the *why*. To help them see that while we may not always have a ton, we always have something to give to help others.

It doesn't have to be money. When you step up and choose to be a generous person of heart and spirit, you can probably change more lives than you ever could with money. It goes much deeper than that. Taking time to truly get to know people. In conversation, being interested in the other person, being intentional, remembering how many children they have, or what they might be struggling with. Being there with them when they're celebrating good times and supporting them when they hit a rough patch. Not judging or looking down upon anyone. They could be *you* given different circumstances, experiences, and upbringings. You can serve people just by learning who they really are over who you assumed them to be.

Take the time to actually care, to actually listen. To look eye-to-eye with your fellow man and recognize the value in them they may not see themselves. Serve people by being there for them, however you can. If you can't give an extra-big tip to the Uber driver who tells you they're saving up to visit their family yet, just listen…. wholly hear them. Ask questions and follow-up questions. Give someone a hug if they need it. Help with a major project that's holding them back. Be interested and intentional in the lives of others. Even those you may not meet again. I still remember my wife laughing at me for taking the time to laugh with the resident of a lone open toll booth one particularly busy night while we were dating. I looked at the attendant as I passed her my coins. Her weariness oozing out of her like a wet sponge. Exhausted by the dozens of cars in line sharing their annoyance that she was the only one there and that they'd been inconvenienced by the long delay. I took one look and told her that I bet she felt like a "superhero" and that I was *so* glad she was there. She responded slowly at first and then a very honest grin lined her face before she laughed. She felt valued instead of berated. Understood instead of annoyed.

We all need more of that these days… I left with a smile imprinted on my heart that will stay with me forever.

"When your values are clear to you, making decisions becomes easier."

Roy E. Disney

"I have learned that as long as I hold fast to my beliefs and values - and follow my own moral compass - then the only expectations I need to live up to are my own."

Michelle Obama

"A mission statement is not something you write overnight... But fundamentally, your mission statement becomes your constitution, the solid expression of your vision and values. It becomes the criterion by which you measure everything else in your life."

Stephen Covey

Chapter 11

Personal Core Values

When you are going about life with little to no personal direction, adrift in the sea of possibilities, or feeling alone in the mire of depressive introspection; I find it far too easy to miss out on opportunities. You lose so much when you choose not to take care of *yourself*.

If you have no clear purpose, no core values, no intentional standards by which you live, you lose out on what comes from holding true to your innate self. You lose the opportunity to fully value your experience in life in discovering what it means to you.

"Crafting thoughtful and meaningful core value statements is critical to long-term growth strategy." - Verne Harnish, *Scaling Up*

Establishing and following meaningful core values, enables you to truly chase after *real* life. Choosing adventure, or being a servant to others, teaches you to understand yourself, to value every moment's experience. Whatever it is about you that creates the building blocks for your personality, you need to know *what* they are. You need to take time for self-reflection, and to really, truly value *who* you are. You need to study yourself, how you're living in your life, and how it affects the lives of those around you.

So many people don't want to take responsibility for how things are going in their lives. Instead, they look at life as something that happens "to them." *Reject this myth.* Accept your responsibility for everything you do. Accept that while you are not always growing, you *always* hold the reins to your future – no matter what happens in your world.

One of my favorite sayings is that truly healthy and wealthy people never say they "haven't had time" for something, rather, they admit they "haven't *made* time" for it. They *own* their reality.

Find out who you are today, who you want to be tomorrow, and what values you need to hold to live that life. What kinds of values are you going to embrace? Selfishness or selflessness? Self-focused or community based? Self-limiting fearfulness or adventurous self-belief?

The Power of Knowing Yourself

Self-care is critical in having the energy to achieve your goals and dreams, as well as having what it takes to support those you love. Self-care starts by knowing your true self, and your true self's values. The book *The Road Back to You* by Ian Morgan Cron and Suzanne Stabile outlines this very nicely; they describe "ignorance is bliss – except in self-awareness." In the very first chapter the authors discuss how everyone wears a mask. These masks can differ, depending on who we're in front of. Most of us wear a different mask for our mother-in-law, employees or employer, spouse, children, and friends.

The book focuses on the Enneagram, a model of human personality types. According to Cron and Stabile, the very first mask you put on as a child is your *personality*. Who were you before your personality? Who were you before you felt you had to adapt to the needs and expectations of others? Who is that core person? It's this concept which is behind the Enneagram numbers discussed in the book, and it's something that has really opened my own eyes to myself, and those around me.

There are many personality profile tests you can take, the Enneagrams mentioned above, the DISC test, Myers-

Briggs, etc. The more you know about yourself, the more you can live within what you learn about yourself. We keep a library of books available for our employees so they can learn about what makes them tick, and how they can fit into the organization. I've found that people who live positively within their personality, within constructive and meaningful core values, life in general seems to happen more easily for them than it does for those who live negatively.

My wife and I have largely had a strong relationship through the years, but knowing deeper specifics about ourselves, via the Enneagram, have helped transform how we understand each other. We better comprehend our go-to patterns and habits, helping each other better expand our capabilities. My wife is a "two" in the Enneagram system, so she has a naturally self-effacing personality, always inclined to serve others, putting her own needs and value to the side. Knowing this about her helps me ensure I'm not putting more on her plate than she can manage. I constantly remind her of just how important it is that she practice self-care and value her own needs as highly as those of others… because without her filling her own cup, she cannot forever fill others.

I'm a "social" seven. Driven not only to constantly seek pleasant experiences and to "silver linings" negative experiences, but I'm even more driven to ensure that any one I care about experiences nothing but the happiest of things as well. My personal challenge is a deeply held lack of personal boundaries, of self-belief that my experience is not as valuable as those I love.

Decisions we make are driven by our inner needs, and our inner self, which is why I've invested so much time into investigating who I am at my core and will continue to do so throughout my life. I've found diving into this type of exploration is not only worth the time and energy, it's crucial to understanding both the ways we consistently make mistakes and what will truly fulfill us. It's worth it to explore who you are by reading books, attending workshops, and doing the work needed to really understand who you are now – and who you can be.

Only then can you develop core values that make sense for you, based upon what you discover about *yourself*. When you've done that deep self-examination, it can enable you to finally become who you're meant to be.

Start With Why

Simon Seneck's remarkable book turned Ted Talk, turned sensation, *Start With Why*, talks about the importance of understanding the core mission and value of what you're doing in life and in business. He talks about different brands that focus their energies on the *why* of their products instead of just focusing on what they do.

Learning about yourself isn't just about reading a book or taking a test. Taking adventures, putting yourself in uncomfortable, sometimes painful, circumstances forces you to ask the all-important *"why."* Why did you travel there? What is it you're missing? What were you looking for when you created this radical experience for yourself?

When I was getting to know my wife's mother as an adult (my wife and I grew up together, so her mother knew child me quite well), she once quietly said, "You know yourself better than anyone else I know." At the time, I had only begun to explore myself and my core values as deliberately as I do now, but I frequently look back to that day as the first one where I acknowledged the true power and freedom of understanding my personal *why.*

Thinking about the "why" barely crossed my mind as we rode our motorcycles day after day in the pouring rain in Alaska, our bodies cold to the point of shaking near uncontrollably, with no distractions, no one to talk to, nothing to challenge me except my own mind. On one such day, during this grand adventure, we made it just eight miles after riding from sunup to sundown. In the moment, I never even stopped to ask… "Why am I doing this?" But hundreds of times since then, I've queried myself; What drew me to that challenge? To surmount ice covered mountain passes? To explore glaciers in the rain? Or to accept the kindness of strangers along the way?

The answer to each of those detailed questions isn't as important as the heart of the problem.

Why am I, the way I am?

The act of asking *that* question, and looking at yourself, is a type of self-reflection many don't take the time to examine. But, in doing so, you can form your core values and your direction. Knowing your "why" forces you to keep pushing, shows how strong you are, and not only what you're made of physically and emotionally now, but who you can strive to be.

Mosquito in a Nudist Colony

Throughout my childhood, my parents were speakers at the homeschool conferences where we sold our massive stock of books. During one of the favorite moments in his speech, my father used to refer to me following my interests as a "mosquito in a nudist colony:" constantly shifting my focus, being drawn to new and exciting things. So many things interested and motivated me. I *had* to learn more. I had to understand everything I possibly could. ADD, ADHD, whatever initials you wanted to give it, I was a rapid learner. One driven to absorb as much as possible in as little time as necessary.

Even if you don't have the *"Uncommon Gift"* (a great book by James S. Evans) of ADD, knowing your "why" *may* change, but the way you choose to *live* your "why" should continue to be childlike – with absolute passion and reckless abandon. It doesn't mean you should put your life in danger, but you must look at everything you do and choose to do it with passion, zeal, and as if it *matters*. Because if you are choosing to live life wholly, it truly does matter. We're offered such a short time here in this life. Choosing to do anything but soak up every moment of it, living without really *living* is an empty, even selfish act. Whether you are sweeping floors or flying, fully choosing to live with purpose and joy inspires you to easily discover and follow your core values.

Big decisions may not necessarily come easily when you are honoring your core, but by using your values as a lens to constantly look through you can question, "Does this honor who I am meant to be?" There are no *"maybes,"* just simple "yes" or "no" answers.

My core values are:

- Serving others.
- Staying positive.
- Trusting people.
- Living in gratitude and joy.

I ask myself, when faced with any decision, "Does this positively or negatively affect my values of living life in joy? In being grateful? Am I in service to others in a positive way?"

If the answer is no, there is no answer but to move to a better place. A place that *builds* upon my values.

Taking Time to see the Butterflies

As a practice, I push myself to take a few minutes each day without my phone, without my computer, without any people around, or any other distractions, and take time to ground myself. To just look at the view. Imagined or real. Picturing a place I'm grateful for in my mind. Watching the sunset perhaps, being quiet, still, and learning to find yourself and understand your core truth. I've pushed myself into some serious personal discomfort (at least when I first started this) by working to follow a guided meditation each day. Usually led by one of the men I truly respect in how aware he is of himself, Luke Gifford (*masterheart.com*). Pushing myself beyond the flurry of what's happening in the now, and just *being* with my inner self, has been truly transformational. I ask myself, "How am I living toward my truth, my *inner* core's values?"

This practice has helped so much when painful times hit, as they inevitably do, and it's *most* important to hold to those moments of optimism and joy.

When my brother passed, I was tasked with going through the thousands of pictures we had of him and his twenty two-year life. I wept as I went through box after box,

Facebook, and camera rolls, going through so many photographs of my brother, living his life fully, gone all too soon.

After many hours of this, I realized a pattern that brought me to tears once again (for perhaps the five hundredth time that week). I found dozens and dozens of pictures of my brother with butterflies. A butterfly on his finger when he was just four or five. Then again as a young man with one perched upon his motorcycle helmet as he sat emanating pure joy. Another butterfly sat on his shoulder in a park on a beautiful spring day. It was a supernatural reminder to focus on the positive. Those butterflies and their beauty dance in my mind. Perfectly in step with the wonderful life my brother led. Now, when any one in our family sees butterflies, we see the beauty of the life James lived and we *know* his joy is with us.

"He who would learn to fly one day must first learn to stand and walk and run and climb and dance; one cannot fly into flying."

Friedrich Nietzsche

"The most difficult thing is the decision to act, the rest is merely tenacity. The fears are paper tigers. You can do anything you decide to do. You can act to change and control your life; and the procedure, the process is its own reward."

Amelia Earhart

"As we fly, we still may not know where we are going to. But the miracle is in the unfolding of the wings. You may not know where you're going, but you know that so long as you spread your wings, the winds will carry you."

C. JoyBell C.

Chapter 12

Doing Something Superhuman

As a child, I remember my parents pointing out buzzards soaring above the ground, flying in tight circles, seemingly in place. They told me these birds were either circling the dead or looking for their next meal. For years, that was my assumption as well… but we were so ill-informed.

Birds of all types and sizes ride thermic currents of air high into the sky, not out of necessity, but because they love it! I've now had the honor of sharing thermals with great blue herons flying alongside cattle egrets and hawks more than 6,000 feet in the sky. On one occasion, I remember climbing slowly to cloud base on my paramotor, engine off for over an hour scratching for lift as I followed bird after bird, trusting their intuition. Suddenly I found myself flanked on either side by a pair of striking bald eagles. Nearly close enough for me to brush their wings with my fingertips, they peered at me long and hard enough to feel as if we had a special moment together. Slowly, we made eye contact in what I believe was a show of mutual respect and acknowledgment of each other's presence and joy.

In our lives, so often we are overwhelmed by the day to day struggles it's easy to just not acknowledge it. It feels beyond our abilities, both physically and emotionally. We are constantly barraged by so many problems, stresses, so much information and pressure; life can feel like "too much" very quickly.

But, when you're flying, you can't be overwhelmed. The minute you feel that way, you're relying on hope, and frankly, there's *no room* for hope in aviation. In flight, we have to learn how to make decisions quickly, how to internalize natural reactions, understand the risks, and move to solutions quickly.

Overcoming "Overwhelm"

Once, I was flying home from my family's favorite getaway, Dog Island. It's a small spit of sand in the Gulf of Mexico where my grandparents invested $35,000 back in the 1960s to buy a small cottage on the bay side. I was with my brother, Joseph, ducking under and over a series of thunderstorms that confounded our journey. In my Van's RV-6, we found ourselves flying lower and lower to avoid being sucked into the dangerous clouds. At nearly 200 miles-per-hour, things happen fast. Pushed by the weather, we were flying so low we were constantly on the lookout for passing towers, and I knew we had to divert and land at an airport that didn't have thunderstorms blocking its runways.

We found a hole in the clouds that hosted a perfect airport where we could safely land, take a deep breath, and have a lovely lunch. I knew I could have pushed on, "hoping" we would be ok, but being squeezed between massive storm cells is not just potentially dangerous, it could have killed us and endangered others on the ground. I had to make the decision quickly to land. I couldn't let myself be overwhelmed by the desire to get home, to appease those who needed us there. To satisfy our schedules, to prove flying was better than driving – but most of all, I couldn't *accept* overwhelm in any sense.

Every day, we are faced with what sometimes feels like superhuman problems, but are they? I believe we are given *just* what we are meant to have on our plate. Solely what we alone can handle. At times the pain from my past injuries has blinded me and I have forced myself to think, not "why me?" but instead "I'm glad this is for me, because while it hurts, while it cripples, I know I am *made* to handle this. What if it happened to someone else I love? I don't want to see them go through this…. *I was made for it.*"

Flying *is* superhuman. We're not born capable of being high up in the sky. However, we overcome what we think are limitations, and the greatest among us literally shoot for the stars.

Getting to that point doesn't come instantly. To master paramotoring takes years and years; just to launch takes internalizing and automating more than thirty different elements, intuitions, decisions, and actions, many of which happen simultaneously and initially overwhelm the senses. The first purpose of our classes at Aviator is to help students learn they cannot accept their natural state of overwhelm in those moments. To remind them that when they choose to, they hold the power over their minds and bodies to become *more*, and to take those first delicate steps into the sky.

Anything that brings you to a place of immense fulfillment and satisfaction is going to come with challenges. Challenges that you, in your current understanding of yourself, may not be able to overcome. Unless, you set those fears to the side and find the strength within you to move beyond yourself, beyond your fears and self-limiting beliefs.

I mentioned earlier in this book the challenge of moving from a place of comfort to a place of discomfort. Students all the time tell us how learning to fly has helped them do so. How they have opened their eyes to higher potential and purpose. I hear from spouses and parents of students all the time about how much their loved one's life has changed through the process of learning to fly. I've watched, first-hand, flight change life after life. Taking the most easily angered, frustrated individual and leaving them with a divine sense of calm; the most anxious, socially awkward are transformed into inspired leaders who transfix entire rooms of people – urging them to better their own lives just like they have. Flying, living wholly, doing something superhuman, opens us up to become who we were *meant* to be – *who we were born to be.*

Step by Step

So often we look at a big task, goal, or vision and think it impossible. And, it *is* impossible to complete it in just one step. But, if we can break it down into first steps, second steps, third steps, and so on, forward movement is *everything.* It builds our confidence and assures we know our path.

No one learns to fly by being thrown in a harness and told, "Ok, here we go, fly!" No, we break it down, long before you run into the sky.

First, you learn to control the glider. Then, to control the motor. Next to control the motor in the air. Then, how to control the glider in the air. Finally, we tie it all together, along with a plethora of ground school knowledge and understanding. When it's all done, you not only have a wealth of information, but we've helped you master flight through practice and positivity. To master anything, you have to listen, trust in the process, and most importantly you have to work hard to get out of your own way.

Every time I land after paramotoring or paragliding, I crack a genuine smile and let out a whole-hearted laugh. Often I find myself giggling like a schoolgirl. I'm elated, happy, and overwhelmed by the purist joy. Every time I step into the sky, *each* flight is somehow better than the last. When we step into what feels like impossible situations or circumstances, and we land on our feet, that overwhelming feeling of elation shows us we have accomplished something bigger than ourselves.

This chapter might be misnamed – it's not about being superhuman, it's about being who you're *meant* to be. It's about being who you were created to be, instead of who you've been, and who you've become, living within fear instead of faith. Learn to confront the challenges of your life instead of running from them. When you do, you *will* feel a peace which can't be counterfeited.

Fear and Faith

Skydiving was one of my first great loves in flight. At a certain point in each jump, there is a magical moment as you reach terminal velocity. Air flows freely around you. Your nerves suddenly relax. No longer just falling, you feel as if you're flying…you're one with the space around you. It's a peaceful existence as you take in all of the world below.

Living in faith instead of fear incites that same deep feeling of freedom. I believe fear and faith are the antithesis of one another. For everything we live in fear of, we are outside of faith in. Faith in ourselves. Faith in those around us. Faith in God or whatever higher power you believe in. Faith in humanity.

Anything we take on in fear deeply affects us negatively. It stands in direct opposition to the faith we should be holding toward life. Our fear clashes completely with the happy, *whole* place where we're meant to be.

"I believe every human has a finite number of heartbeats. I don't intend to waste any of mine."

Neil Armstrong

"The line between life or death is determined by what we are willing to do."

Bear Grylls

"Endurance is patience concentrated."

Thomas Carlyle

Chapter 13

Endurance; Going the Distance

One of the things I love about paramotoring is how deeply every flight is recorded in your subconscious. Even years later you can call each one back at any time. Every moment of every flight – it's almost like having a TiVo in your brain. You can remember what you smelled. You can remember what it felt like.

One year, I was in the Czech Republic for ten days, and each day we went on a new, wild flying adventure. We were there to visit a factory for a paramotor brand I was selling at the time, staying in an old Russian Air Force base. There were giant gray bunkers everywhere, it was both bleak, and industriously beautiful. Early each morning we would take off and fly for two or more hours, downwind to a new adventure. As visitors on the trip, we never knew where we would end up, and our hosts didn't know much English.

"We go there!" they would yell out, pointing to the horizon and each of us would then follow the fastest guy. Hours of flying over the most incredible places. Worlds away from the coldness of the Russian base. Czech Republic has some of the most diverse countryside I've ever seen, and it was amazing to take it all in, I was enthralled with each different direction and destination. One day it would feel like we were flying in the south of France. The next, Switzerland. It was incredible.

Picture yourself cruising down a mountain pass, going over mountain range after mountain range, high in the air. As you climb, you overfly snow-capped mountains, looking straight down between your feet to see little villages that seem completely lost in time. Popping over the next mountain ridge you're suddenly flying over a gorgeous, glistening white castle, transfixed by the flags waving from the battlements. After diving down the mountainside you climb over the next and suddenly see a dozen fellow paramotorists readying to take off with you and experience this adventure together.

One day we landed at a winery, had our fill of homemade sausages and wine, staying the night in the onsite hostel. The next day, flying home we experienced a completely different world of countryside and history. Different castles, antiquated radio towers, and power stations belching mist into the air sunk into my treasure trove of memories as my friends and I flew around them all. Enjoying laughter from farmers as we swept across their fields of grain, watching the wake turbulence from our motors move them as if by an unseen hand.

Enduring Pain and Heartache

It sounds like heaven, and in many ways it was, but the pain I experienced due to my former injuries was monumental. By the time we ended each flight, the pain was almost unbearable. My legs would shake uncontrollably from applying speedbar (a method of increasing our forward speed by twenty to thirty percent) for hours at a time. Landing with the heavy motor on my back and having to hike to our pickup location felt next to impossible some days, but I *had* to persevere if I wanted to keep experiencing the joy and elation I received whenever I flew. I couldn't allow my discomfort to restrain me. There were rally car races to view from above! New cities to visit, new mountainsides to speed down. I had to keep going.

The amount of resiliency you find within yourself and within those you choose to surround yourself with can be incredible. Each of those flights, along with others I've experienced all over the world, have refined who I am through their hardships. Being willing to take on the pain, the challenge, and continue despite the struggle is my greatest reward. I could have landed early. I could have skipped a day. I could have not flown when I hurt. But where is the benefit in taking the easy way out? In choosing to be the victim?

Sure, it hurt… so much sometimes it took my breath away, but I wasn't causing any long-lasting damage to my body, and the reward made every physical pain *worth* it. There was a guy in our group who only flew once the trip. He had some challenges during his first flight and opted out of every further adventure. Each day I thought about what he was missing out on. I chose to never be *that* guy. I chose to take the risk, weather the pain, and experience real *adventure*.

If you've had some type of mishap, mustering up the courage to keep moving forward can be hard, but your rewards *always* multiply. The guy who only flew once gave up because he had run out of fuel the first day. He let the fear of repeated problems overcome him, instead of taking simple steps to ensure they didn't happen again. It wasn't that he was physically unable to fly – his brain simply mustered up enough fear of failure that he missed out on all the joy.

This was a man who had more years of flying experience than I had at the time but he chose the "comfortable" path, spending the week sitting in the back of the van, driving around the countryside that I was entranced flying over and through. But, was he safe? Was he free? Was he truly living?

Life is Short - Shed Complacency

If you haven't yet, read a copy of *Jonathan Livingston Seagull*, a truly classic book written in the late 1960s by Richard Bach. One of my favorite quotes from the book is, "*Jonathan Seagull discovered that boredom and fear and anger are the reasons that a gull's life is so short, and with these gone from his thought, he lived a long fine life indeed.*"

Endurance in life is not just about putting up with something long enough, or persevering through pain, it's about recognizing that everything you do in this moment, on this day, may very well impact what happens in one year, two years, even a decade from now. Understanding and recognizing we should always think about the long distance run we're all undertaking. Sometimes opportunities don't come your way until you're ready for them. Until you've built yourself, your skills – your actual *self* – to be ready for them.

Endurance ensures you still *work*, still put in the time and effort to get where you want to go. If things don't fall in your lap, it's not that it's not meant to be, perhaps the time isn't quite right – maybe you're not ready physically, emotionally, or spiritually. Each day, we are given *exactly* what we were created to handle.

I try to help my children see that no matter how hard things might seem at the moment for them, at the end of the day, their world is okay and all they have to do is overcome their frustrations and move through their emotions to see the truth of their situation. They have to choose joy over their natural anger and victimization. They have to choose joy instead of choosing to remain injured. Throughout my trip to the Czech Republic, I faced that hundred-pound motor every morning, questioning if I had the strength to carry it to the point of launch.

But, every day I did it. I picked the motor up, I ached, I struggled, and I felt the pain attack my back. Yet, the moment my feet left the ground, I experienced a massive sense of relief and accomplishment. *Oh my God, I did it!* I thought to myself each time. I endured, beyond the pain, the jet lag, and the weariness, beyond my fears and the scars of my past trauma. I *chose* to endure.

Breaking Down "Insurmountable" Tasks and Goals

When I was twelve, my family hiked Yosemite National Park. At the time, it seemed insurmountable, and in many ways for me it was. I was asthmatic, built like a twig, and was in no way an outdoorsman. My head more often found in a book or magazine rather than pushing myself forward physically. Initially I was convinced I would *never* make it to the top of even the most relatively simple hike. But, something in me mustered me the wisdom to realize; if I thought about it a little differently, I could do it. Instead of thinking of the whole trail, I would think, *I just have to get past that tree*, or *I just have to get around the bend*.

By breaking it down into little missions and challenges anyone could easily handle, I was able to complete each hike, and make it back *triumphant*! Today, breaking goals down into bite-sized chunks is *still* how I tackle big challenges. Even though the journey may be long and difficult, I know I can make it by taking it one step at a time.

"The joy of life consists in the exercise of one's energies, continual growth, constant change, the enjoyment of every new experience. To stop means simply to die. The eternal mistake of mankind is to set up an attainable ideal."

Aleister Crowley

"Strength and growth come only through continuous effort and struggle."

Napoleon Hill

"Without continual growth and progress, such words as improvement, achievement, and success have no meaning."

Benjamin Franklin

Chapter 14

Constant Growth

I've had lots of interests and hobbies pass through my life, from surfing, to building race cars, and riding motorcycles. All of them have fallen off the map because over time I've reached a certain level of success, and it's enough. But, with flying there's never been a moment of, "*I've made it.*" Every flight is a new opportunity to enhance and improve at something – even if it's something small.

I find myself finding something to perfect every flight. For example, working on exactly when I should throw my weight to the opposite side of the harness of my Parajet Maverick paramotor to begin the next loop of a barrel roll. I used to shift early, slowing the glider before it reached its maximum velocity. Through slow experimentation, I've learned to wait – literally just a few tenths of a second – and it makes a world of difference in how my rolls look, *and* feel.

There's always something I can push and grow with flight. Whether it's landings, takeoffs, rolls, footdrags, or cross country planning. There's always a detail I can learn to better and perfect, as long as I'm willing to put in the practice and exercise the patience that doesn't come naturally to me.

In life we often look at problems as being single entities, instead of looking at them, and life, as segmented processes. Alternatively, looking at the past year's successes and challenges together, learning to recognize patterns or things that can be done better the next year, and the next, and the next, until each life skill is perfected. With paramotors, every single movement and decision you make affects how the craft flies. When you take a closer look, the same is true in all of our lives.

We get to choose how we have conversations with our loved ones, our colleagues, or friends, and neighbors. We get to consider each conversation as a building block. If we break each into smaller and smaller elements we can more directly tackle and perfect them. Just like flight, where the tiniest moment can affect the greater experience, these tiny elements can be practiced and perfected.

Only by breaking things down beyond considering them "grand issues" can we refine the process of how we live. Think of the elite sprint runner who trains for hours, days, weeks, and months to get a hundredth of a second better at their skill. As an observer, you might never notice their improvement, let alone think about how it relates to their drive to continuously improve, but they see it and they know its value.

Perfecting Life by Pursuing Joy

I believe part of perfecting life is finding and pursuing what you really enjoy. You can perfect *nearly* any skill with enough effort, but if your heart isn't in it, you won't stick with it long enough. I remember as a child being taught to play piano via the Suzuki method. After over two years of lessons (which I abhorred), I found myself still playing "Twinkle, Twinkle Little Star," in all its variations. Piano didn't inspire me. I felt constantly setup for failure and some part of me didn't see the pay off.

But each of us are so very different. My wife is a concert pianist with nearly two decades of professional training and a deep desire to continue her growth. She learned to play the pipe organ beautifully, an incredible feat on its own, but then decided to take up the cello as well. She still plays *something* on a near daily basis. She feels music like I feel flight. She feels the need to perfect each note, convey each composer's vision, and most of all, to keep pushing herself forward with each movement she plays.

Each of us must find satisfaction in the *process* of whatever we're doing. Without fascination in the job at hand, along with having a genuine sense of satisfaction, you'll never *fully* perfect any skill worth having. You're always growing. As we grow, our next goal appears. Often, we see in our clients something unfulfilled, a drive to be *whole.* On the surface it may be through learning how to fly, but I believe it's deeper than that. They see that there is more to who they are meant to be.

We get people who scuba dive, fly airplanes, sail boats, race cars, build all sorts of crazy things, and more; each an attempt to find the piece in their soul that is missing. For many people, those single activities fulfill them. If just for a time. Many of our clients have found flying takes the place of any other activity they've pursued in hopes of fulfilling their heart's desire to truly live. Flying *becomes* them.

Flying brings out a special type of peace with its natural – supernatural – sense of *true* freedom. Our students tell us they finally feel they're not encumbered or held back. They've left behind the sensation of feeling blocked, stuck, or even moving backwards. They are free to fly, literally, as well as emotionally and spiritually.

Find Your Joy - Join Everything

When you find any one thing that might be your adventure, you have to tackle it. You have to *try.* Personally, I've lived with an idea that's helped guide my decisions: "Five years from now, if I do this, and it goes horribly wrong, will it still matter? Will it injure those I care about, or damage my future?" If not, I take the plunge. I move forward in faith, rather than fear.

Instead, I've been able to go after something I've dreamed of, added an incredible life experience, and maybe, just maybe, found something that truly inspires me. Something I was willing to step forward in faith to truly experience.

I remember having a conversation with my wife when she was feeling frustrated. I was working on growing our three businesses at the time. I had hobbies, interests, and passions (going back to the "mosquito in a nudist colony" reference from my dad – it's just how I'm wired). She held herself back at the time, not being as hard wired to encourage herself to experience new adventures. She was talking about wanting something new to inspire her but didn't know where to start. I told her simply, "Try everything!"

"Join every group, join every club, try everything you think you might be even remotely interested in. Go volunteer. Get an unusual job. Anything that might bring joy to you. Anything that might drive you. Go! Live! Find yourself through living and continually trying."

After recognizing this genuine need for more in her life, my wife took to the skies for the first time as a certified paramotor pilot. Throughout my life of personal flight, she's been a bystander. She's supported me through everything but has been focused on being the caretaker for our children, either pregnant, or nursing throughout most of my adventure. Three years prior she told me she was ready to learn. But early in the spring of 2019 she told me she was ready to *fly*. We put her on the schedule for class immediately… and on the fifth of November, she took to the skies. I've never been more proud of her. Overcoming the physical challenges, the mental. Arriving at a new level of herself she didn't even know was within her.

Yet, too many people are afraid to change lanes. It can be scary to shift out of your place of comfort, but I've seen the rewards of doing just that. My brother, Joseph, was a police officer for six years, he loved his job and was great at it. Officer of the year, SWAT team member, sniper team leader, more accolades and commendations than almost anyone could expect to receive in such a short tenure. But what he loved more was being a "Three Gun" competitor and firearms instructor. It took a huge move to leave behind his pensioned, cautious plan, but now he's operating at the highest level of who he was meant to be. He was even selected for Team USA, and they took second at the IPSC World Rifle Championship in Sweden and even won the Three Gun Nationals in Las Vegas. He is constantly booked as an instructor, all over the world. He stepped out of his "secure" full-time income to pursue his passion in a radical way. His confidence has paid off. He now can profit in a day what he used to make in two weeks or more.

Another dear friend is also a first responder. He's grown to hate much of his work – he's great at it, don't get me wrong – but he's miserable in the position. I've begged him to quit, to take a chance and do something else with his life. The man is immensely talented! Yet he keeps saying to me, "A few more years before my retirement." I tell him it's not just a few more years, it's years of being miserable and unhappy. In those years, he *could* transform his life.

We're granted nothing in life more fleeting and valuable than the time we have here. Using it for anything but the things that make us come most genuinely alive, the things that inspire us to bless others, is a personal tragedy for each of us. I've fallen down those rabbit holes myself. Those moments of believing I should continue doing something because I've started it, only to discover it's not something worthy. It can be so, so difficult to step away. But the time we have here is so precious, we MUST think beyond ourselves, we must consider those we love, and chase the life we *might* have if we fully embraced faith in what we know we should be. If we fully embrace how much more fulfilled we might become, we will thus fulfill others all the more.

It's not security if it's killing your soul.

"I am not fearless. I get scared plenty. But I have also learned how to channel that emotion to sharpen me."

Bear Grylls

"The most fearless hearts, the audacious dreamers, have always maintained a sense of optimism that often flies in the face of the available evidence."

Martin O'Malley

"Fearlessness is not only possible, it is the ultimate joy. When you touch nonfear, you are free."

Thich Nhat Hanh

Chapter 15

Pushing Past Fear and Doing What You Hate

Learning to fly paramotors was the hardest thing I've had to do in my life – physically, emotionally, even spiritually. It left me on the dirt, exhausted and miserable, so many times.

I spent my first days learning to fly at a school run very differently than what I now consider ideal. With ancient equipment in a terribly challenging location, I experienced endless frustrations. The physical pain of the heavy equipment that incited in my back felt like a railroad spike piercing my spine and leaving me crippled by the end of every day.

In my first six months of flying, I went to the field, laid out my glider, then tried to launch, finally leaving the ground the sixth or seventh time. In between those attempts, I laid on the ground, drenched in sweat, experiencing pain so intense I don't have the right words to describe it.

I hated it at first.

Yet, what was born from that was a tenacity I didn't know I had. I refused to let this beat me. It was hard. It hurt. It was frustrating. I had only two flights under my belt when I "completed" my training.

I went home, not knowing any better, and went to fly. I took the glider to the field, laid it out, and after several attempts finally launched. I was elated when my feet left the ground and I took to the air. At first, the joy outweighed everything else, and I felt genuine joy at overcoming the odds, at finding myself airborne. But soon enough, oscillations began and I started swinging side to side.

My instructor had taught me how to fix this but looking back I realize now he taught me an incomplete fix. He told me to "come off the power and let it settle." Now that would work in some situations, but it was not the best choice at 100 feet and with equipment set up improperly to handle the torque. Instead, I found myself oscillating out of control, and rushing toward the ground before taking blackberry bushes to the face.

Brambles and thorns stuck to my legs, my arms, and my face. I had hundreds of scrapes and scratches on each of my appendages. I laid there, soaked in aviation fuel as it poured down my back, and thought to myself, *Holy cow, I could have died.*

But a few minutes later, no other option available to me, I laid the glider in the middle of the field once again, took off, and flew back to the airport. When I got back, I called my wife on the drive home and warned her, "Honey, I'm fine, but I don't look fine." I walked through the door of our home, covered in blood, stinking of fuel, and full of pride that I'd *finally* made not just one, but two, launches on my own. Needless to say, she was shocked, but knowing who I am she understood when I declared, "I *have* to get back and keep learning."

I flew every flyable day that year. Hundreds of hours, because I had a drive to overcome and not let it beat me. Through all the pain. Through all the sweat. Through all the occasions that reminded me of my first accident, laying on the ground hating myself for my previous injuries, but unwilling to give in – or give up. I learned the struggle was more than worth it.

As I fell in love with the sport and it became something I *had* to do. It quickly became my life. Already a fixed wing ultralight instructor, I soon found myself teaching people the early steps to fly a paramotor, and with that, my love for the sport grew even further. I saw how it could affect others as it had affected me. How it could allow them to push past their fears and pains. Watching them as they landed from their first flights quickly became an aphrodisiac as I saw how real their joy was.

The rest is history.

The Things We Hate are the Things We Fear

Take a look in the mirror – literally or figuratively. Is there a part of you which you hate? Even despise? Outside of things not in your control, like your outward appearance, what is it about yourself you don't like, that you wish you could change, but perhaps you're afraid to address?

It could show itself as mundane things, like when I put off taking my test to become a licensed pilot. It wasn't just that I hated taking tests, it was because I was afraid of seeing myself as a failure.

By deliberately taking on tasks we may not enjoy, that may cause fear in us, we learn and grow beyond anything we can imagine. After getting my license, I gave myself the challenge of becoming an instrument rated pilot – the obvious next step in my growth. It's all about learning procedures, math, and precision. Things that make my right brained personality cry out with angst. There's nothing in the process of studying for the test that does anything to fill me with joy… that is, until I complete it.

The honest reason for being overfilled with joy after an accomplishment is because of the knowledge that I went through the mundane hardship and personal fears of failure intentionally. I chose this path, and I refuse to quit. I choose to become a better person through it, because I want to be able to safely travel with my family through uncertain conditions I wouldn't otherwise be able to without that type of knowledge. With each step I take toward bettering myself, I know I will be able to better support not just myself, but those I love.

I choose to press on now and will continue to for the rest of my life – overcoming and growing through every single experience.

Finding Something That Intimidates You

When we choose to be intimidated by something, and then choose to make it a non-factor, we are choosing discomfort to ultimately achieve joy. When we knock down our challenges one by one, they no longer act as a negative factor in our lives. We choose to say, "This is something that might be traumatizing and trying for me, but I'm going to go through it."

By doing this, you become the person you are supposed to be. If, instead, you allow things like this to

overcome you, you cut who you were meant to be short of
who you can be.

Crashing my paramotor into that thorny bush ultimately motivated me. It intimidated me on each of my next flights, but I didn't let myself fall into the victim mentality. Instead, I researched torque compensation, oscillation control, and I asked more experience pilots for help, coming to them in humility with my desire to grow. *Always* working to surpass the natural overwhelm that comes from unexpected hardship.

Owning Failure and Success

If there's one thing I really want readers to get out of this book, it's to look at the fact that *we* are in command of how we react to life. We can choose to live in fear, or, we can choose to live strong.

There are a lot of us who become the victim because we blame someone outside of ourselves. We blame external forces for our difficulties. But, if we look at our experiences as a series of *internal* forces, we can *conquer* what's inside us. That's the difference. To own failure and success is to never blame someone else. The instructor who incorrectly taught me how to deal with oscillations isn't the reason I failed. Ultimately, I chose not to fail because I knew I had the capability to succeed through my own willingness to own my failures, to humble myself. Through it all I ended up owning my success. Running into the sky once again, just minutes after my disgrace.

We had a student who had some challenges in his initial training. Everything happened *"to him."* He never engaged with anyone in his class, didn't put forth any real effort, and his wingman had to do all the work. He became one of our most challenging clients, to the point we offered a full refund for everything just to try and please him. He received our offer and angrily turned it down, stating we were just trying to make him the villain.

In that moment, he chose to be the victim, the martyr. He chose to blame everyone else for his failure and didn't take any responsibility for his role of his inability to have a good experience. He didn't try to overcome his fears or have faith in himself. The hard part for me has been letting go of my desire to help him more than he helped himself. I know this is part of his journey. Someday, maybe he'll realize *he has* control, that he can be the victor over his circumstances, and grow to be the man he has always wanted to be.

Letting go of Victimhood

This client's story is rare in that he never shed the notion of victimhood through the training process. More often than not, when clients come into our school with similar attitudes. They're looking to fill some kind of life gap they perceive comes from some force external to their control, however they learn, in addition to flight, how to *own* failures and successes. How to shed the notion that things happen *to* them.

It happens quickly in our schools because they almost instantly see how their actions have reactions. How a slight change in how they hold their posture, arms, or attitude alters their success. They then have to react, to adjust. They have to correct and learn how to do it without rushing, panicking, becoming aggravated, or shutting down. These responses have to become second nature to truly succeed.

We teach that everyone's successes are each other's successes, and everyone's failures are each other's failures. We'll hear on the field when someone takes their first flight, instructors and students cheering, clapping, and whistling. And, when everyone lands from their first flight, the whole group runs up to give them the world's most awkward hug because of the gangly motor on their back.

It's beautiful because we grow together and we choose to lift each other up. When we have those rare clients who come in and can't push past their victim-based mentality, we've learned it's better if we give them the opportunity to leave, head held high. We give up the financial success we would have otherwise because we don't want to pollute how they are going to affect everyone around them. We see all too clearly that only those who are *ready* to grow will ever do so.

"Life is too short to eat dessert last." - Trent Palmer

We are always moving – growing or dying – we set our own stage for that movement. Forward, back, or not at all. Build your own speedometer. And by God, know you are worthy of one that has no negative numbers. There is too much good, too much greatness laid out before you, to live any life that is less than epic. I am excited for your journey.

Final Thoughts

Life is too easy to lose quickly. It only takes a second. We can barely count on tomorrow. We can plan all we want, but reality is that no one gets out alive. Our power comes from choosing to make our life as joyful and fulfilling as we possibly can. We choose how we live, for ourselves and for those we love. If we were to leave this earth tomorrow, what kind of mark would we want to leave on our world and on those around us?

In this book, I've talked about my life in relation to learning to fly, in learning to choose adventure and to relish in the growth brought to us by discomfort. The experiences I've shared here directly relate to how I have chosen to live my life, and I hope they have inspired you to look at your own life in a new way, to see how you can continue growing yourself, and the lives of those around you.

Life is fragile. Choosing to do what you love is important, even over what you're most successful at. By focusing on your passions, you *will* be more successful and whole in the long run. Living your passions can and often will wash over into all the spokes of your world; relationships, financial security and wealth, emotional, physical well-being, social success, and spiritual peace.

I remember the time, day, and moment I decided to give up my successful career in marketing. I had just closed my biggest sales day ever and was soaking it up in the hot tub under the stars of a Texas sky with my newly wedded wife.

She looked at me with pain in her eyes and said, "You should quit, you hate this."

"What are you talking about? I love this?" I replied, sipping on a glass of wine and soaking up every beautiful moment.

"No, you hate this – you're miserable and you're in pain. You should quit, do photography, and fly. Do what you love."

It took a while to see the truth she saw. I'd worked for nearly a decade to accomplish what my mentors had done. To speak from the stage, share my dreams, and make sales at the end of it. But she was right. I had grown my abilities, had helped a lot of people, but by the end of each conference my stress and emotional pain had grown to such levels it was as if my subconscious was screaming to be heard. I was good at what I was doing, and I had created a lot of fiscal success, but I was absolutely miserable. The only reward was the money, and it just wasn't enough. My soul was hurting.

I made the decision right then and there to liquidate the business and pursue my dreams.

I challenge you to shed your skin – frequently. If you're comfortable, I dare you to make yourself uncomfortable. I encourage you to pursue what you love and learn from what you fear.

One of the things I do every day, when I see my children in the evening, is ask them what it is they were grateful for that day. What is it *you're* grateful or? What do you still want to achieve in life? Where can you improve to become the person you were born to be?

Whatever it is, go to the field, lay your glider out, check your equipment, and *fly*!

"Fear is the glue that keeps you stuck.
Faith is the solvent that sets you free"

Shannon L. Addler

"Success cannot be measured in wealth,
fame, or power, but by whether you have
made a positive difference for others."

Sir Richard Branson

Thank You For Reading My Book!

Through the process of writing this, I've relived many adventures long forgotten, reminded myself of beliefs that had settled into my subconscious, and have been challenged constantly by each sentence. I've questioned whether or not my story is *worthy* of being shared. The discomfort has been *real*.

But, if you're here now; I believe it's all been worth it. I hope my words turn a key inside your mind. That they inspire you to look beyond your current self and focus your attention on what *could* be just over the next hill. I hope you can look at yourself with pride, knowing that you're doing the hardest part *right now*. Taking time to work to better yourself is never easy. But here you are. I am so honored by the gift of your time and attention.

As you finish this book, I hope you take a step forward in your life. You may already know which steps are needed first. Whatever *your* path, I truly hope to fly with you someday soon.

If this book has inspired you to look skyward, or you'd just like to keep up with our Aviator family, you can find us at the links below:

www.AviatorParamotor.com
www.EricFarewell.com

www.Facebook.com/AviatorPPG
www.YouTube.com/Aviator
www.instagram.com/AviatorShow
www.instagram.com/AviatorParamotor
www.instagram.com/AviatorFamily

If you're ready to learn more about learning to fly, discover more details at:

www.AviatorPPG.com/training

I'm hopeful you've enjoyed this book. If you have, please take the time to not just write a review on Amazon, but also to pay it forward and share this book with someone you feel might be blessed by it.

Thank you for going on this journey with me.

I am honored,

Eric

About the Author:

Eric Farewell is a lifelong adventurer, entrepreneur, and lover of life. He is the father of three children, one dog, and husband to one wife. He is hopelessly addicted to all things that go "vroom," yet (secretly an introvert) his favorite vacations include mountains, books, and no expectation to move off the couch.

Eric passionately encourages people to overcome their fears through flight. He believes his team at Aviator Paramotor are some of the best humans to ever walk the earth and he feels honored to have your interest in his book. You can follow Eric's adventures at: http://youtube.com/Aviator.

Eric sharing his "truest joy" face with the sky on his
Paramotor.

Eric and Danielle, "Nelle," his wife of over ten years in their vintage Piper Cub.

Eric, after test flying an airplane in northern California, at age 17.

On the Bow Tie Tour, Eric and his friend Ethan Demme are

beginning the Alcan Highway. Age, 19.

Crossing the border into Alaska felt like a monumental
moment for them on the Bow Tie Tour.

Eric and a student "bowling" at a competition in the airplane
that would eventually break his back. Age, 17.

After restoring this 1970 VW, Eric drove it from LA to Seattle
and back, surfing along the way. Only sinking it in the Pacific
once before making it home safely. Age, 22.

Eric loving being *in* the sunset over his home airport of Lake Wales.

Eric's 1946 Piper Cub.

Celebrating New Year's at home with young children meant funny hats for Eric, Nelle, and his brother James in 2014.

A favorite photo of Eric's family. Nelle, August, Arthur, and Eloise. Circa 2017.

A capstone moment, flying in front of the St. Louis Arch July 4th, 2018

Enjoying the skies of Montana.

Eric on his 2001 Yamaha FZ-1 at 19 years old. En route to Alaska.

One of the many lodges on the route to Alaska. It was a place like this where they met Sean Penn.

Florida skies will always be one of Eric's favorite places to be

The Paradigm Aerobatic Team at AirVenture. Oshkosh 2017

The Aviator and Paradigm family Airventure, Oshkosh 2017.

Eric's 1947 Cessna 120.

Eric sharing one of his favorite books from childhood with his own children, August and Arthur.

Eric and Nelle on their first flight together after *finally* receiving
his pilot's license in 2017.

Eric and Nelle after her first solo flight… completed during the writing of this book in 2019.

.

www.ingramcontent.com/pod-product-compliance
Lightning Source LLC
Chambersburg PA
CBHW070335220526
45467CB00001B/135